W9-CIL-690

CCNP ISCW
Portable Command Guide

Scott Empson
Hans Roth

Cisco Press

800 East 96th Street
Indianapolis, IN 46240 USA

CCNP ISCW Portable Command Guide

Scott Empson, Hans Roth

Copyright © 2008 Cisco Systems, Inc.

Published by:
Cisco Press
800 East 96th Street
Indianapolis, IN 46240 USA

Printed in the United States of America

First Printing   March 2008

Library of Congress Cataloging-in-Publication Data

Empson, Scott.
  CCNP ISCW portable command guide / Scott Empson, Hans Roth.
    p. cm.
  ISBN 978-1-58720-186-8 (pbk.)
  1. Computer networks--Problems, exercises, etc. 2. Computer networks--Examinations--Study guides. 3. Packet switching (Data transmission)--Examinations--Study guides. I. Roth, Hans. II. Title.

  TK5105.8.C57E57 2008
  004.6--dc22

                                    2008004857

ISBN-13: 978-1-58720-186-8
ISBN-10: 1-58720-186-0

This Book Is Safari Enabled

The Safari® Enabled icon on the cover of your favorite technology book means the book is available through Safari Bookshelf. When you buy this book, you get free access to the online edition for 45 days.

Safari Bookshelf is an electronic reference library that lets you easily search thousands of technical books, find code samples, download chapters, and access technical information whenever and wherever you need it.

To gain 45-day Safari Enabled access to this book:

- Go to http://www.informit.com/onlineedition.

- Complete the brief registration form

- Enter the coupon code STFG-Q1KG-224L-GNGP-JWE9

If you have difficulty registering on Safari Bookshelf or accessing the online edition, please e-mail customer-service@safaribooksonline.com.

Warning and Disclaimer

This book is designed to provide information about the Cisco Certified Network Professional (CCNP) Implementing Secure Converged Wide Area Networks (ISCW) exam (642-825) and the commands needed at this level of network administration. Every effort has been made to make this book as complete and as accurate as possible, but no warranty or fitness is implied.

The information is provided on an "as is" basis. The authors, Cisco Press, and Cisco Systems, Inc., shall have neither liability nor responsibility to any person or entity with respect to any loss or damages arising from the information contained in this book or from the use of the discs or programs that may accompany it.

The opinions expressed in this book belong to the authors and are not necessarily those of Cisco Systems, Inc.

Trademark Acknowledgments

All terms mentioned in this book that are known to be trademarks or service marks have been appropriately capitalized. Cisco Press or Cisco Systems, Inc., cannot attest to the accuracy of this information. Use of a term in this book should not be regarded as affecting the validity of any trademark or service mark.

Corporate and Government Sales

The publisher offers excellent discounts on this book when ordered in quantity for bulk purchases or special sales, which may include electronic versions and/or custom covers and content particular to your business, training goals, marketing focus, and branding interests. For more information, please contact: **U.S. Corporate and Government Sales** 1-800-382-3419   corpsales@pearsontechgroup.com

For sales outside the United States, please contact: **International Sales** international@pearsoned.com

Feedback Information

At Cisco Press, our goal is to create in-depth technical books of the highest quality and value. Each book is crafted with care and precision, undergoing rigorous development that involves the unique expertise of members from the professional technical community.

Readers' feedback is a natural continuation of this process. If you have any comments regarding how we could improve the quality of this book, or otherwise alter it to better suit your needs, you can contact us through e-mail at feedback@ciscopress.com. Please make sure to include the book title and ISBN in your message.

We greatly appreciate your assistance.

Publisher	Paul Boger
Associate Publisher	Dave Dusthimer
Cisco Representative	Anthony Wolfenden
Cisco Press Program Manager	Jeff Brady
Executive Editor	Mary Beth Ray
Managing Editor	Patrick Kanouse
Development Editors	Chris Cleveland, Dayna Isley
Senior Project Editor	San Dee Phillips
Copy Editor	Bill McManus
Technical Editor	Neil Lovering
Editorial Assistant	Vanessa Evans
Cover and book Designer	Louisa Adair
Composition	Octal Publishing, Inc.
Proofreader	Leslie Joseph

CISCO SYSTEMS

Corporate Headquarters	European Headquarters	Americas Headquarters	Asia Pacific Headquarters
Cisco Systems, Inc.	Cisco Systems International BV	Cisco Systems, Inc.	Cisco Systems, Inc.
170 West Tasman Drive	Haarlerbergpark	170 West Tasman Drive	Capital Tower
San Jose, CA 95134-1706	Haarlerbergweg 13-19	San Jose, CA 95134-1706	168 Robinson Road
USA	1101 CH Amsterdam	USA	#22-01 to #29-01
www.cisco.com	The Netherlands	www.cisco.com	Singapore 068912
Tel: 408 526-4000	www-europe.cisco.com	Tel: 408 526-7660	www.cisco.com
800 553-NETS (6387)	Tel: 31 0 20 357 1000	Fax: 408 527-0883	Tel: +65 6317 7777
Fax: 408 526-4100	Fax: 31 0 20 357 1100		Fax: +65 6317 7799

Cisco Systems has more than 200 offices in the following countries and regions. Addresses, phone numbers, and fax numbers are listed on the
Cisco.com Web site at www.cisco.com/go/offices.

Argentina • Australia • Austria • Belgium • Brazil • Bulgaria • Canada • Chile • China PRC • Colombia • Costa Rica • Croatia • Czech Republic
Denmark • Dubai, UAE • Finland • France • Germany • Greece • Hong Kong SAR • Hungary • India • Indonesia • Ireland • Israel • Italy
Japan • Korea • Luxembourg • Malaysia • Mexico • The Netherlands • New Zealand • Norway • Peru • Philippines • Poland • Portugal
Puerto Rico • Romania • Russia • Saudi Arabia • Scotland • Singapore • Slovakia • Slovenia • South Africa • Spain • Sweden
Switzerland • Taiwan • Thailand • Turkey • Ukraine • United Kingdom • United States • Venezuela • Vietnam • Zimbabwe

About the Authors

Scott Empson is the associate chair of the bachelor of applied information systems technology degree program at the Northern Alberta Institute of Technology in Edmonton, Alberta, Canada, where he teaches Cisco routing, switching, and network design courses in a variety of different programs—certificate, diploma, and applied degree—at the post-secondary level. Scott is also the program coordinator of the Cisco Networking Academy at NAIT, a Regional Academy covering central and northern Alberta. He has earned three undergraduate degrees: a bachelor of arts, with a major in English; a bachelor of education, again with a major in English/language arts; and a bachelor of applied information systems technology, with a major in network management. He currently holds several industry certifications, including CCNP, CCAI, and Network+. Prior to instructing at NAIT, he was a junior/senior high school English/language arts/computer science teacher at different schools throughout northern Alberta. Scott lives in Edmonton, Alberta, with his wife Trina and two children Zachariah and Shaelyn, where he enjoys reading and training in the martial art of tae kwon do.

Hans Roth is an instructor in the Electrical/Electronic Engineering Technology department at Red River College in Winnipeg, Manitoba, Canada. Hans has been with the college for 11 years and teaches in both the electronic technology and IT areas. He has been with the Cisco Networking Academy since 2000, teaching CCNP curricula. Previous to teaching Hans spent 15 years in R&D/product development designing microcontroller-based control systems for consumer products as well as for the automotive and agricultural industries.

About the Technical Reviewer

Neil Lovering, CCIE No. 1772, works as a design consultant for Cisco. Neil has been with Cisco for more than three years and works on large-scale government networking solutions projects. Prior to Cisco, Neil was a network consultant and instructor for more than eight years and worked on various routing, switching, remote connectivity, and security projects for many customers all over North America.

Dedications

This book is dedicated to Trina, Zach, and Shae, without whom I couldn't have made it through those long nights of writing and editing.

—Scott Empson

I'd like to dedicate this book to my wife Carol and daughter Tess. I am thankful for their grace and patience with me during my many hours in the basement.

I'd also like to dedicate this book to my wife Carol. I'm hopeful two dedications are worth more than one.

—Hans Roth

Acknowledgments

Anyone who has ever had anything to do with the publishing industry knows that it takes many, many people to create a book. Our names may be on the cover, but there is no way that we can take credit for all that occurred in order to get this book from idea to publication. Therefore, we must thank:

From Scott Empson: To the team at Cisco Press, once again you amaze me with your professionalism and the ability to make me look good. Mary Beth, Chris, Patrick, Drew, San Dee, Bill, and Dayna—thank you for your continued support and belief in my little engineering journal.

To my technical reviewer, Neil, thanks for keeping me on track and making sure that what I wrote was correct and relevant.

To the staff of the Cisco office here in Edmonton, thanks for putting up with me and my continued requests to borrow equipment for development and validation of the concepts in this book.

A big thank you goes to my coauthor, Hans Roth, for helping me through this with all of your technical expertise and willingness to assist in trying to make my ideas a reality.

From Hans Roth: I don't exactly know how many people it takes to get a book on the shelf. The content must be written, the graphics drawn, each section verified technically, each part massaged in editing, the presentation layout manipulated and re-edited, and the pre- and post-press work completed, including the many marketing efforts. Of course, this process includes the organization and patience of the editor and editorial staff. Certainly, the writing part is only one effort in a large collection of efforts.

To the Cisco Press team, thank you for your patience and guidance—especially you, Mary Beth.

To the technical reviewer, Neil Lovering—thanks.

Lastly I would like to thank my colleague in education and cowriter, Scott Empson. Scott's boundless energy has helped me refocus when I needed to. Scott's positive attitude, tempered with his vast experience in education and technical areas, was an excellent rudder to help me stay on course. Finally, Scott's experience with the process of writing for Cisco Press saved me from many of the "newbie" writer foibles. Thank you Scott for freely sharing your experience with me.

Contents at a Glance

Contents

Icons Used in This Book

PC

Router

Workgroup
Switch

Firewall

PIX Firewall

DSLAM

File Server

Access
Server

IP Phone

Cisco 5500
Family

VPN
Concentrator

Modem

Command Syntax Conventions

The conventions used to present command syntax in this book are the same conventions used in the *IOS Command Reference*. The *Command Reference* describes these conventions as follows:

- **Boldface** indicates commands and keywords that are entered literally as shown. In actual configuration examples and output (not general command syntax), boldface indicates commands that are manually input by the user (such as a **show** command).

- *Italics* indicate arguments for which you supply actual values.

- Vertical bars (l) separate alternative, mutually exclusive elements.

- Square brackets [ ] indicate optional elements.

- Braces { } indicate a required choice.

- Braces within brackets [{ }] indicate a required choice within an optional element.

Introduction

Welcome to ISCW! In 2006, Cisco Press contacted Scott and told him, albeit very quietly, that there was going to be a major revision of the CCNP certification exams. They then asked whether he would be interested in working on a command guide in the same fashion as his previous books for Cisco Press: the Cisco Networking Academy Program *CCNA Command Quick Reference* and the *CCNA Portable Command Guide*. The original idea was to create a single-volume command summary for all four of the new CCNP exams. However, early on in his research, Scott quickly discovered that there was far too much information in the four exams to create a single volume—that would have resulted in a book that was neither portable nor quick as a reference. So, Scott jokingly suggested that Cisco Press let him author four books, one for each exam. Well, you have to be careful what you wish for, because Cisco Press readily agreed. Realizing that this was going to be too much for one part-time author to handle, Scott quickly got his colleague Hans Roth on board as a coauthor.

This book is the third in a four-volume set that attempts to summarize the commands and concepts that you need to understand to pass one of the CCNP certification exams—in this case, the Implementing Secure Converged WANs exam. It follows the format of Scott's previous books, which are in fact a cleaned-up version of his own personal engineering journal—a small notebook that you can carry around that contains little nuggets of information such as commands that you tend to forget, the IP addressing scheme of some remote part of the network, and little reminders about how to do something you need to do only once or twice a year that is vital to the integrity and maintenance of your network.

With the creation of two brand-new CCNP exams, the amount of new information out there is growing on an almost daily basis. There is always a new white paper to read, a new Webinar to view, another slideshow from a Networkers session that was never attended. The engineering journal can be that central repository of information that won't weigh you down as you carry it from the office or cubicle to the server and infrastructure room in some branch office.

To make this guide a more realistic one for you to use, the folks at Cisco Press have decided to continue with an appendix of blank pages—pages on which you can write your own personal notes, such as your own configurations, commands that are not in this book but are needed in your world, and so on. That way this book will look less like the authors' journals and more like your own.

Networking Devices Used in the Preparation of This Book

To verify the commands in this book, many different devices were used. The following is a list of the equipment used in the writing of this book:

- C2620 router running Cisco IOS Release 12.3(7)T, with a fixed Fast Ethernet interface, a WIC-2A/S serial interface card, and an NM-1E Ethernet interface
- C2811 ISR bundle with PVDM2, CMME, a WIC-2T, FXS and FXO VICs, running Cisco IOS Release 12.4(3g)
- C2821 ISR bundle with HWICD 9ESW, a WIC-2A/S, running 12.4(16) Advanced Security IOS
- WS-C3560-24-EMI Catalyst switch, running Cisco IOS Release 12.2(25)SE
- WS-C3550-24-EMI Catalyst switch, running Cisco IOS Release 12.1(9)EA1c
- WS-C2960-24TT-L Catalyst switch, running Cisco IOS Release 12.2(25)SE
- WS-C2950-12 Catalyst switch, running version C2950-C3.0(5.3)WC(1) Enterprise Edition software
- C1760 1FE VE 4SLOT DV Mainboard Port adapter with PVDM2, CMME, WIC-2A/S, WIC-4ESW, MOD1700-VPN with 32F/128D running c1700-bk9no3r2sy7-mz.124-15.T1

- C1751 1FE VE DV Mainboard with WIC-4ESW, MOD1700-VPN with 16F/64D running c1700-advsecurityk9-mz.124-5a
- Cisco 3640 with 32F/128DRAM memory, 3 Ethernet interfaces, 2-WIC-1T running c3640-jk9o3s-mz.124-12a

These devices were not running the latest and greatest versions of Cisco IOS Software. Some of the equipment is quite old.

Those of you familiar with Cisco devices will recognize that a majority of these commands work across the entire range of the Cisco product line. These commands are not limited to the platforms and IOS versions listed. In fact, in most cases, these devices are adequate for someone to continue their studies beyond the CCNP level.

Who Should Read This Book

This book is for those people preparing for the CCNP ISCW exam, whether through self-study, on-the-job training and practice, study within the Cisco Networking Academy, or study through the use of a Cisco Training Partner. There are also some handy hints and tips along the way to make life a bit easier for you in this endeavor. This book is small enough that you will find it easy to carry around with you. Big, heavy textbooks might look impressive on your bookshelf in your office, but can you really carry them all around with you when you are working in some server room or equipment closet somewhere?

Organization of This Book

This book follows the list of objectives for the CCNP ISCW exam:

- **Chapter 1, "Network Design Requirements"**—Offers an overview of the two different design models from Cisco: the Service-Oriented Network Architecture and the Enterprise Composite Network Model
- **Chapter 2, "Connecting Teleworkers"**—Describes how to provision a cable modem, and how to configure a Cisco router as a PPPoE client
- **Chapter 3, "Implementing Frame Mode MPLS"**—Describes how to configure MPLS on a router, including configuring CEF, configuring MPLS on a frame mode interface, and configuring MTU size in label switching
- **Chapter 4, "IPsec VLANs"**—Describes how to configure, verify, and troubleshoot IPsec VLANs, including topics such as configuring IPsec, configuring GRE tunnels, creating High Availability using HSRP and stateful failover, Cisco Easy VPN Server and client, and configuring Easy VPN Server using Cisco SDM
- **Chapter 5, "Cisco Device Hardening"**—Includes topics such as locking down routers with AutoSecure; setting login failure rates, timeouts, and multiple privilege levels; Role-Based CLI; securing your configuration files; and configuring SSH servers, syslog logging, NTP clients and servers, and AAA
- **Chapter 6, "Cisco IOS Threat Defense Features"**—Includes topics such as configuring a basic firewall from the CLI and SDM, configuring a DMZ, and configuring inspection rules as part of an Advanced Firewall

Did We Miss Anything?

As educators, we are always interested to hear how our students, and now readers of our books, do on both vendor exams and future studies. If you would like to contact either of us and let us know how this book helped you in your certification goals, please do so. Did we miss anything? Let us know. Contact us at ccnpguide@empson.ca.

This chapter provides information concerning the following topics:

- Cisco Service-Oriented Network Architecture
- Cisco Enterprise Composite Network Model

No commands are associated with this module of the CCNP ISCW course objectives.

Cisco Service-Oriented Network Architecture

Figure 1-1 shows the Cisco Service-Oriented Network Architecture (SONA) framework.

Figure 1-1   Cisco SONA Framework

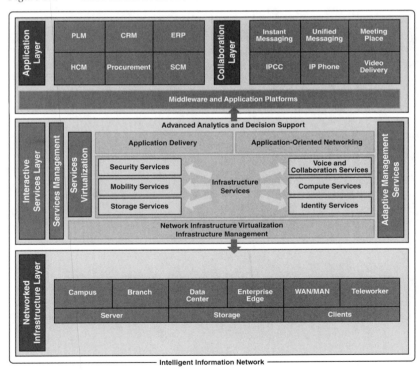

Cisco Enterprise Composite Network Model

Figure 1-2 shows the Cisco Enterprise Composite Network Model.

Figure 1-2   *Cisco Enterprise Composite Network Model*

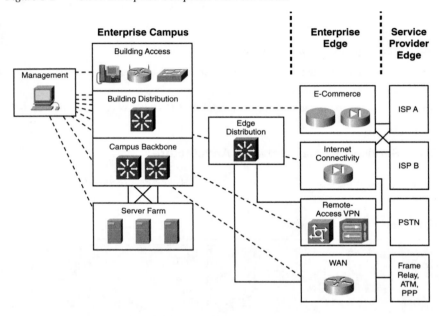

CHAPTER 2

Connecting Teleworkers

This chapter provides information and commands concerning the following topics:

- Configuration example: DSL using PPPoE
  - Basic router configuration
  - Understanding VPDN
  - Declaring PPPoE at the physical interface
  - Negotiating PPPoE addressing
  - Adjusting packet sizes
  - Creating a dialer interface
  - Declaring PPP at the logical dialer interface
  - Choosing "interesting" dialer traffic
  - Verifying PPPoE and PPP
- Configuring PPPoA
- Configuring a cable modem connection
  - Connection using an external cable modem
  - Bridging the cable and Ethernet interfaces (internal modem)
- Configuring L2 bridging using a Cisco cable modem HWIC
- Configuring L3 routing using a Cisco cable modem HWIC
  - Routing a Cisco cable modem HWIC and Ethernet interface

Configuration Example: DSL Using PPPoE

Figure 2-1 shows an asymmetric digital subscriber line (ADSL) connection to the ISP DSL address multiplexer.

Figure 2-1   PPPoE Reference Topology

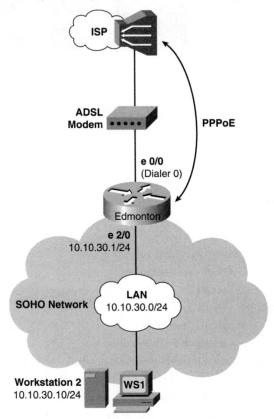

The programming steps for configuring Point-to-Point Protocol over Ethernet (PPPoE) on an Ethernet interface are as follows:

Step 1.   Configure PPPoE (external modem).

Step 2.   Configure the dialer interface.

Step 3.   Define interesting traffic and specify default routing.

Step 4a.   Configure Network Address Translation (NAT) using an access control list (ACL).

Step 4b.   Configure NAT using a route map.

Step 5.   Configure Dynamic Host Configuration Protocol (DHCP) service.

Step 6.   Apply NAT programming.

Step 7.   Verify a PPPoE connection.

Step 1: Configure PPPoE (External Modem)

Edmonton(config)#**interface ethernet0/0**	Enters interface configuration mode
Edmonton(config-if)#**pppoe enable**	Enables PPPoE on the interface
Edmonton(config-if)#**pppoe-client dial-pool-number 1**	Chooses the physical Ethernet interface for the PPPoE client dialer interface
Edmonton(config-if)#**no shutdown**	Enables the interface
Edmonton(config-if)#**exit**	Returns to global configuration mode

Virtual Private Dial-Up Network (VPDN) Programming

Edmonton(config)#**vpdn enable**	Enables VPDN sessions on the network access server
Edmonton(config)#**vpdn-group** *PPPOE-GROUP*	Creates a VPDN group and assigns it a unique name
Edmonton(config-vpdn)#**request-dialin**	Initiates a dial-in tunnel
Edmonton(config-vpdn-req-in)#**protocol pppoe**	Specifies the tunnel protocol
Edmonton(config-vpdn-req-in)#**exit**	Exits request-dialin mode
Edmonton(config-vpdn)#**exit**	Exits vpdn mode and returns to global configuration mode

NOTE: VPDNs are legacy dial-in access services provided by ISPs to enterprise customers who chose not to purchase, configure, or maintain access servers or modem pools. A VPDN tunnel was built using Layer 2 Forwarding (L2F), Layer 2 Tunneling Protocol (L2TP), Point-to-Point Tunneling Protocol (PPTP), or Point-to-Point over Ethernet (PPPoE). The tunnel used UDP port 1702 to carry encapsulated PPP datagrams and control messages between the endpoints. Routers with Cisco IOS Release 12.2(13)T or earlier require the additional VPDN programming.

Step 2: Configure the Dialer Interface

Edmonton(config)#**interface dialer0**	Enters interface configuration mode
Edmonton(config-if)#**ip address negotiated**	Obtains IP address via PPP/IPCP address negotiation
Edmonton(config-if)#**ip mtu 1492**	Accommodates for the 6-octet PPPoE header to eliminate fragmentation in the frame
Edmonton(config-if)#**ip tcp adjust-mss 1452**	Adjusts the maximum segment size (MSS) of TCP SYN packets going through a router to eliminate fragmentation in the frame
Edmonton(config-if)#**encapsulation ppp**	Enables PPP encapsulation on the dialer interface
Edmonton(config-if)#**dialer pool 1**	Links the dialer interface with the physical interface Ethernet 0/1 **NOTE:** The ISP defines the type of authentication to use.

For Password Authentication Protocol (PAP)

Edmonton(config-if)#**ppp authentication pap callin**	Uses PAP for authentication
Edmonton(config-if)#**ppp pap sent-username** *pieman* **password** *bananacream*	Enables outbound PAP user authentication with a username of **pieman** and a password of **bananacream**

For Challenge Handshake Authentication Protocol (CHAP)

Edmonton(config-if)#**ppp authentication chap callin**	Enables outbound CHAP user authentication
Edmonton(config-if)#**ppp chap hostname** *pieman*	Submits the CHAP username
Edmonton(config-if)#**ppp chap password** *bananacream*	Submits the CHAP password
Edmonton(config-if)#**exit**	Exits programming level

Step 3: Define Interesting Traffic and Specify Default Routing

Edmonton(config)#**dialer-list** 2 **protocol ip permit**	Declares which traffic will invoke the dialing mechanism
Edmonton(config)#**interface dialer0**	Enters interface mode
Edmonton(config-if)#**dialer-group** 2	Applies the "interesting traffic" rules in **dialer-list 2**
Edmonton(config)#**ip route 0.0.0.0 0.0.0.0 dialer0**	Specifies the dialer0 interface as the candidate default next-hop address

Step 4a: Configure NAT Using an ACL

Edmonton(config)#**access-list 1 permit 10.10.30.0 0.0.0.255**	Specifies an access control entry (ACE) for NAT
Edmonton(config)#**ip nat pool NAT-POOL 192.31.7.1 192.31.7.2 netmask 255.255.255.0**	Defines the inside global (WAN side) NAT pool with subnet mask **NOTE:** When a range of public addresses is used for the NAT/PAT inside global (WAN) addresses, it is defined by an address pool and called in the NAT definition programming.
Edmonton(config)#**ip nat inside source list 1 pool NAT-POOL overload**	Specifies the NAT inside local addresses by ACL and the inside global addresses by address pool for the NAT process **NOTE:** In the case where the inside global (WAN) address is dynamically assigned by the ISP, the outbound WAN interface is named in the NAT definition programming.
Edmonton(config)#**ip nat inside source list 1 interface dialer0 overload**	Specifies the NAT inside local addresses (LAN) and inside global addresses (WAN) for the NAT process

Step 4b: Configure NAT Using a Route Map

Edmonton(config)#**access-list 3 permit 10.10.30.0 0.0.0.255**	Specifies the access control entry (ACE) for NAT
	NOTE: The **route-map** command is typically used when redistributing routes from one routing protocol into another or to enable policy routing. The most commonly used method for defining the traffic to be translated in the NAT process is to use an ACL to choose traffic and call the ACL directly in the NAT programming. When used for NAT, a route map allows you to match any combination of ACL, next-hop IP address, and output interface to determine which pool to use. The Cisco Router and Security Device Manager (SDM) uses a route map to select traffic for NAT.
Edmonton(config)#**route-map ROUTEMAP permit 1**	Declares route map name and enters route-map mode
Edmonton(config-route-map)#**match ip address 3**	Specifies the ACL that defines the dialer "interesting traffic"
Edmonton(config-route-map)#**exit**	Exits route-map mode
Edmonton(config)#**ip nat inside source route-map ROUTEMAP interface dialer0 overload**	Specifies the NAT inside local (as defined by the route map) and inside global (interface dialer0) linkage for the address translation

Step 5: Configure DHCP Service

Edmonton(config)#**ip dhcp excluded-address 10.10.30.1 10.10.30.5**	Excludes an IP address range from being offered by the router's DHCP service
Edmonton(config)#**ip dhcp pool CLIENT-30**	Enters dhcp-config mode for the pool CLIENT-30
Edmonton(dhcp-config)#**network 10.10.30.0 255.255.255.0**	Defines the IP network address
Edmonton(dhcp-config)#**default-router 10.10.30.1**	Declares the router's vlan10 interface address as a gateway address
Edmonton(dhcp-config)#**import all**	Imports DHCP option parameters into the DHCP server database from external DHCP service **NOTE:** Any manually configured DHCP option parameters override the equivalent imported DHCP option parameters. Because they are obtained dynamically, these imported DHCP option parameters are not part of the router configuration and are not saved in NVRAM.
Edmonton(dhcp-config)#**dns-server 10.10.30.2**	Declares any required DNS server address(es)
Edmonton(dhcp-config)#**exit**	Exits dhcp-config mode

Step 6: Apply NAT Programming

Edmonton(config)#**interface ethernet2/0**	Enters interface mode
Edmonton(config-if)#**ip nat inside**	Specifies the interface as an inside local (LAN side) interface

`Edmonton(config)#`**`interface dialer0`**	Enters interface mode
`Edmonton(config-if)#`**`ip nat outside`**	Specifies the interface as an inside global (WAN side) interface
`Edmonton(config-if)#`**`end`**	Returns to privileged EXEC mode

Step 7: Verify a PPPoE Connection

`Edmonton#`**`debug pppoe events`**	Displays PPPoE protocol messages about events that are part of normal session establishment or shutdown
`Edmonton#`**`debug ppp authentication`**	Displays authentication protocol messages such as CHAP and PAP messages
`Edmonton#`**`show pppoe session`**	Displays information about currently active PPPoE sessions
`Edmonton#`**`show ip dhcp binding`**	Displays address bindings on the Cisco IOS DHCP server
`Edmonton#`**`show ip nat translations`**	Displays active NAT translations

Configuring PPPoA

The programming steps for configuring PPP over ATM (PPPoA) on an ATM interface are as follows:

Step 1.   Configure PPPoA on the WAN Interface (Using Subinterfaces)

Step 2.   Configure the dialer interface.

Step 3.   Verify a PPPoA connection.

> **NOTE:** The remaining programming is the same as the PPPoE programming.

Step 1: Configure PPPoA on the WAN Interface (Using Subinterfaces)

`Edmonton(config)#`**`interface atm0/0`**	Enters interface mode
`Edmonton(config-if)#`**`bundle-enable`**	Enables multiple PVCs on the interface
`Edmonton(config-if)#`**`dsl operating-mode auto`**	Automatically detects the DSL modulation scheme that the ISP is using
`Edmonton(config-if)#`**`interface atm0/0.1`** **`pointtopoint`**	Creates virtual ATM point-to-point subinterface
`Edmonton(config-if)#`**`pvc 1/2`**	Assigns virtual circuit (VC) 2 on virtual path 1 to the subinterface **NOTE:** **pvc 1/2** is an example value that must be changed to match the value used by the ISP.
`Edmonton(config-if)#`**`dialer pool-member 1`**	Links the ATM interface to the dialer interface
`Edmonton(config-if)#`**`encapsulation aal5mux`**	Configures the ATM adaptation layer (AAL) for multiplex (MUX)-type VCs **NOTE:** The global default encapsulation option is **aal5snap**.

Step 2: Configure the Dialer Interface

`Edmonton(config)#`**`interface dialer0`**	Enters interface mode **NOTE:** When configuring the dialer interface in an ATM environment, it is not necessary to configure the maximum transmission unit (MTU) and adjust the MSS. This is required only when configuring PPPoE.
`Edmonton(config-if)#`**`ip address negotiated`**	Obtains IP address via PPP/IPCP address negotiation
`Edmonton(config-if)#`**`encapsulation ppp`**	Enables PPP encapsulation on the dialer interface
`Edmonton(config-if)#`**`dialer pool 1`**	Links the dialer interface with the physical interface ATM 0/0

For Password Authentication Protocol (PAP)

`Edmonton(config-if)#`**`ppp authentication pap callin`**	Uses PAP for authentication
`Edmonton(config-if)#`**`ppp pap sent-username pieman password bananacream`**	Enables outbound PAP user authentication

For Challenge Handshake Authentication Protocol (CHAP)

`Edmonton(config-if)#`**`ppp authentication chap callin`**	Enables outbound CHAP user authentication
`Edmonton(config-if)#`**`ppp chap hostname pieman`**	Submits the CHAP username
`Edmonton(config-if)#`**`ppp chap password bananacream`**	Submits the CHAP password
`Edmonton(config-if)#`**`exit`**	Returns to global configuration mode

Step 3: Verify a PPPoA Connection

Edmonton#**debug pppatm event vc 1/2**	Displays events on virtual circuit 2 on virtual path 1
Edmonton#**debug pppatm error vc 1/2**	Displays errors on virtual circuit 2 on virtual path 1
Edmonton#**show atm interface atm0/0**	Displays ATM-specific information about an ATM interface
Edmonton#**show dsl interface atm0/0.1**	Displays information specific to the ADSL for a specified ATM interface
Edmonton#**debug ppp authentication**	Displays authentication protocol messages such as CHAP and PAP messages
Edmonton#**show ip dhcp binding**	Displays address bindings on the Cisco IOS DHCP server
Edmonton#**show ip nat translations**	Displays active NAT translations

Configuring a Cable Modem Connection

Figure 2-2 shows a LAN connection and a cable connection to the ISP broadband router.

Figure 2-2   Cable Modem Connection Reference Topology

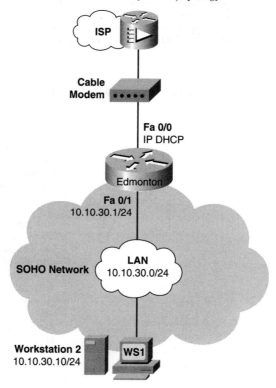

The programming steps for configuring a cable modem connection are as follows:

Step 1.   Configure WAN connectivity

Step 2.   Configure local DHCP service.

Step 3.   Configure NAT using a route map.

Step 4.   Configure default routing.

Step 5.   Apply NAT programming.

> **NOTE:** Connection to a cable system using an external modem is simply a LAN connection with NAT, DHCP, and firewall programming.

Step 1: Configure WAN Connectivity

`Edmonton(config)#interface fastethernet 0/0`	Enters interface configuration mode
`Edmonton(config-if)#no ip route-cache`	Disables fast switching at this interface
`Edmonton(config-if)#no cdp enable`	Disables Cisco Discovery Protocol (CDP) at this interface
`Edmonton(config-if)#mac-address 0017.31c0.9bfa`	Manually sets a MAC address (for authentication purposes) **NOTE:** Some cable service providers use the MAC address of the host PC connected to the cable modem as authentication or link it with the DHCP process. Some cable modems have used the MAC address of their first connected host as the only valid user. Manual configuration of a MAC address at the router/modem interface can solve these problems.
`Edmonton(config-if)#ip address dhcp`	Sets the dynamic addressing as DHCP
`Edmonton(config-if)#no shutdown`	Enables the interface
`Edmonton(config-if)#exit`	Exits interface configuration mode

Step 2: Configure Local DHCP Service

`Edmonton(config)#ip dhcp excluded-address` `10.10.30.1 10.10.30.5`	Excludes an IP address range from being offered by the router's DHCP service
`Edmonton(config)#ip dhcp pool CLIENT-1`	Enters dhcp-config mode for the pool CLIENT-1
`Edmonton(dhcp-config)#import all`	Imports DHCP option parameters into the DHCP server database from external DHCP servicer **NOTE:** Any manually configured DHCP option parameters override the equivalent imported DHCP option parameters. Because they are obtained dynamically, these imported DHCP option parameters are not part of the router configuration and are not saved in NVRAM.
`Edmonton(dhcp-config)#network 10.10.30.0` `255.255.255.0`	Defines the IP network address
`Edmonton(dhcp-config)#default-router` `10.10.30.1`	Declares the router's LAN interface address as a gateway address
`Edmonton(dhcp-config)#dns-server 10.10.30.2`	Declares any required DNS server address(es)
`Edmonton(dhcp-config)#exit`	Exits dhcp-config mode

Step 3: Configure NAT Using a Route Map

Edmonton(config)#**access-list 100 permit ip 10.10.30.0 0.0.0.255 any**	Creates an access list defining which addresses will be translated in the NAT process
Edmonton(config)#**route-map ROUTEMAP permit 1**	Enters route-map configuration mode
Edmonton(config-route-map)#**match ip address 100**	Chooses the access list that defines IP addresses for NAT
Edmonton(config-route-map)#**exit**	Exits route-map configuration mode
Edmonton(config)#**ip nat inside source route-map ROUTEMAP interface fastethernet 0/0 overload**	Specifies the NAT inside local (as defined by the route map) and inside global (interface fastethernet 0/0) linkage for the address translation

Step 4: Configure Default Routing

Edmonton(config)#**ip route 0.0.0.0 0.0.0.0 fastethernet 0/0 A.B.C.D**	Sets the default route to the next-hop address of A.B.C.D

NOTE: Packets from the internal network will be routed to the next hop at A.B.C.D. If interface FastEthernet 0/0 goes down, the route entry will be purged from the routing table and will be reinstated only when interface FastEthernet 0/0 goes back up. If only an outbound interface is specified in the static route, the router believes all destinations to be directly connected and will issue proxy ARP requests. |

Step 5: Apply NAT Programming

`Edmonton(config)#`**`interface fastethernet 0/1`**	Enters interface configuration mode
`Edmonton(config-if)#`**`shutdown`**	Turns off the interface
`Edmonton(config-if)#`**`ip nat inside`**	Defines the interface as an internal interface for the NAT process
`Edmonton(config-if)#`**`no shutdown`**	Enables the interface
`Edmonton(config-if)#`**`interface fastethernet 0/0`**	Enters interface configuration mode for FastEthernet 0/0
`Edmonton(config-if)#`**`shutdown`**	Turns off the interface
`Edmonton(config-if)#`**`ip nat outside`**	Defines the interface as the external interface for the NAT process
`Edmonton(config-if)#`**`no shutdown`**	Enables the interface
`Edmonton(config-if)#`**`exit`**	Exits interface configuration mode
`Edmonton(config)#`**`exit`**	Exits global configuration mode

Configuring L2 Bridging Using a Cisco Cable Modem HWIC

The programming steps for setting up Layer 2 bridging using a Cisco cable modem High-Speed WAN Interface Card (HWIC) are as follows:

Step 1.   Configure global bridging parameters.

Step 2.   Configure WAN to LAN bridging.

Step 1: Configure Global Bridging Parameters

`Router>`**`enable`**	Moves to privileged mode
`Router#`**`configure terminal`**	Enters global configuration mode

`Router(config)#bridge irb`	Enables bridging between routed interfaces and bridge groups
`Router(config)#bridge 59 protocol ieee`	Defines Spanning Tree Protocol
`Router(config)#bridge 59 route ip`	Enables routing of IP in a bridge group

Step 2: Configure WAN to LAN Bridging

`Router(config)#interface bvi 59`	Creates a virtual interface for bridge group 59
`Router(config-if)#interface fastethernet 0/1`	Enters interface configuration mode
`Router(config-if)#no ip address`	Deletes any IP addressing
`Router(config-if)#bridge-group 59`	Assigns bridge group 59 to the interface
`Router(config-if)#interface cable 0/2/0`	Enters interface mode for cable connection
`Router(config-if)#bridge-group 59`	Assigns bridge group 59 to the interface
`Router(config-if)#end`	Returns to privileged modeEnds programming

Configuring L3 Routing Using a Cisco Cable Modem HWIC

The programming steps for setting up Layer 3 bridging using a Cisco cable modem HWIC are as follows:

Step 1.   Remove bridge group programming from all interfaces.

Step 2.   Configure LAN connectivity.

Step 3.   Configure WAN connectivity.

Step 1: Remove Bridge Group Programming from All Interfaces

`Router(config)#`**`interface fastethernet 0/1`**	Enters interface configuration mode
`Router(configif)#`**`no bridgegroup 59`**	Removes bridge group 59
`Router(configif)#`**`no bridgegroup 59 ieee`**	Removes Spanning Tree programming
`Router(configif)#`**`interface cable 0`**	Enters interface configuration mode
`Router(configif)#`**`no bridgegroup 59 ieee`**	Removes Spanning Tree programming
`Router(configif)#`**`no bridgegroup 59`**	Removes bridge group 59
`Router(configif)#`**`exit`**	Returns to global configuration mode

Step 2: Configure LAN Connectivity

`Router(config-if)#`**`interface fastethernet 0/1`**	Creates virtual interface FastEthernet 0/1
`Router(config-if)#`**`ip address`** *`ip address subnet mask`*	Assigns interface address and netmask
`Router(config-if)#`**`no shutdown`**	Enables the interface

Step 3: Configure WAN Connectivity

`Router(config)#`**`interface cable-modem 0`**	Enters interface configuration mode
`Router(config-if)#`**`ip address dhcp`**	Requests IP configuration through DHCP
`Router(config-if)#`**`no shutdown`**	Enables the interface

CHAPTER 3

Implementing Frame Mode MPLS

This chapter provides information and commands concerning the following topics:

- Configuring Cisco Express Forwarding
  - Verifying CEF
  - Troubleshooting CEF
- Configuring MPLS on a Frame Mode interface
- Configuring MTU size in label switching

Configuring Cisco Express Forwarding

To enable MPLS, you must first enable Cisco Express Forwarding (CEF) switching.

> **NOTE:** CEF switching is enabled by default on the following platforms:
> - Cisco 7100 series router
> - Cisco 7200 series router
> - Cisco 7500 series Internet router
>
> dCEF Switching is enabled by default on the following platforms:
> - Cisco 6500 series router
> - Cisco 12000 series Internet router

`Router(config)#ip cef`	Enables standard CEF
`Router(config)#ip cef distributed`	Enables dCEF
`Router(config)#no ip cef`	Disables CEF globally
`Router(config)#interface fastethernet 0/1`	Moves to interface configuration mode
`Router(config-if)#ip route-cache cef`	Enables CEF on the interface

Verifying CEF

`Router#show ip cef`	Displays entries in the forwarding information base (FIB)
`Router#show ip cef summary`	Displays a summary of the FIB
`Router#show ip cef unresolved`	Displays unresolved FIB entries
`Router#show ip cef fastethernet 0/1`	Displays the FIB entry for the specified interface
`Router#show ip cef fastethernet 0/1 detail`	Displays detailed information about the FIB for the interface
`Router#show cef drop`	Displays packets that are dropped due to adjacencies that are incomplete or nonexistent

NOTE: CEF is not supported on logical interfaces, such as loopback interfaces.

Troubleshooting CEF

`Router#debug ip cef`	Displays debug information for CEF
`Router#debug ip cef drop`	Displays debug information about dropped packets
`Router#debug ip cef access-list` *x*	Displays information from specified access lists
`Router#debug ip cef receive`	Displays information about packets received by IP CEF

`Router#debug ip cef events`	Displays general CEF events
`Router#debug ip cef prefix-ipc`	Displays updates related to IP prefix information
`Router#debug ip cef table`	Produces a table showing events related to the FIB table

Configuring MPLS on a Frame Mode Interface

`Router(config)#mpls ip`	Enables MPLS globally on the router **NOTE:** MPLS is enabled by default on Cisco routers. However, if you need to re-enable it, use the global **mpls ip** command.
`Router(config)#interface fastethernet 0/0`	Moves to interface configuration mode
`Router(config-if)#mpls ip`	Enables MPLS on the specified interface
`Router(config-if)#mpls label protocol tdp`	Enables Tag Distribution Protocol (TDP) on this interface **NOTE:** TDP is Cisco proprietary. LDP is a superset of TDP. Cisco is changing from TDP to a fully compliant LDP.

`Router(config-if)#mpls label protocol ldp`	Enables Label Distribution Protocol (LDP) on this interface **NOTE:** LDP is the default protocol on Cisco IOS Release 12.4(3) and later. In older releases, TDP was the default protocol.
`Router(config-if)#mpls label protocol both`	Enables both TDP and LDP on this interface

NOTE: For backward compatibility, the **mpls** syntax will be entered as **tag-switching** syntax in the configuration by the Cisco IOS Software.

Configuring MTU Size in Label Switching

`Router(config)#interface fasthethernet 0/0`	Moves to interface configuration mode
`Router(config-if)#mpls mtu 1512`	Changes the maximum size of an MPLS-labeled packet to 1512 bytes **NOTE:** The **mpls mtu** command is an optional command when working with MPLS. But because of the addition of the label header, the MTU on LAN interfaces should be increased to prevent IP fragmentation. **NOTE:** The minimum MTU is 64 bytes. The maximum MTU depends on the type of interface medium that is being used.

Configuration Example: Configuring Frame Mode MPLS

Figure 3-1 shows the network topology for the configuration that follows, which shows how to configure Frame Mode MPLS using commands covered in this chapter.

Figure 3-1   Network Topology for Frame Mode MPLS Configuration Example

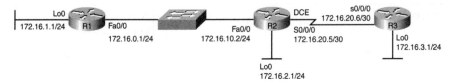

R1 Router

`Router>`**`enable`**	Moves to privileged mode
`Router#`**`configure terminal`**	Moves to global configuration mode
`Router(config)#`**`hostname R1`**	Assigns hostname to router
`R1(config)#`**`ip cef`**	Enables CEF on device (enabled by default)
`R1(config)#`**`mpls ip`**	Enables MPLS globally on device (enabled by default)
`R1(config)#`**`interface loopback 0`**	Moves to interface configuration mode
`R1(config-if)#`**`ip address 172.16.1.1 255.255.255.0`**	Assigns IP address and netmask
`R1(config-if)#`**`interface fastethernet 0/0`**	Moves to interface configuration mode
`R1(config-if)#`**`ip address 172.16.10.1 255.255.255.0`**	Assigns IP address and netmask
`R1(config-if)#`**`mpls ip`**	Enables MPLS on this interface

`R1(config-if)#mpls mtu 1508`	Changes the maximum size of the packet allowed on this interface to 1508 bytes
`R1(config-if)#no shutdown`	Activates interface
`R1(config-if)#exit`	Returns to global configuration mode
`R1(config)#router eigrp 1`	Enables the EIGRP routing process for AS 1
`R1(config-router)#network 172.16.0.0`	Specifies which network to advertise in EIGRP
`R1(config-router)#no auto-summary`	Turns off the auto-summarization feature
`R1(config-router)#exit`	Returns to global configuration mode
`R1(config)#exit`	Returns to privileged mode
`R1#copy running-config startup-config`	Saves configuration in NVRAM

R2 Router

`Router>enable`	Moves to privileged mode
`Router#configure terminal`	Moves to global configuration mode
`Router(config)#hostname R2`	Assigns hostname to router
`R2(config)#ip cef`	Enables CEF on device (enabled by default)
`R2(config)#mpls ip`	Enables MPLS globally on device (enabled by default)
`R2(config)#interface loopback 0`	Moves to interface configuration mode

`R2(config-if)#ip address 172.16.2.1 255.255.255.0`	Assigns IP address and netmask
`R2(config-if)#interface fastethernet 0/0`	Moves to interface configuration mode
`R2(config-if)#ip address 172.16.10.2 255.255.255.0`	Assigns IP address and netmask
`R2(config-if)#mpls ip`	Enables MPLS on this interface
`R2(config-if)#mpls mtu 1508`	Changes the maximum size of the packet allowed on this interface to 1508 bytes
`R2(config-if)#no shutdown`	Activates interface
`R2(config-if)#interface serial 0/0/0`	Moves to interface configuration mode
`R2(config-if)#ip address 172.16.20.5 255.255.255.252`	Assigns IP address and netmask
`R2(config-if)#mpls ip`	Enables MPLS on this interface
`R2(config-if)#clock rate 64000`	Enables clock rate for this interface
`R2(config-if)#no shutdown`	Activates interface
`R2(config-if)#exit`	Returns to global configuration mode
`R2(config)#router eigrp 1`	Enables the EIGRP routing process for AS 1
`R2(config-router)#network 172.16.0.0`	Specifies which network to advertise in EIGRP
`R2(config-router)#no auto-summary`	Turns off the auto-summarization feature
`R2(config-router)#exit`	Returns to global configuration mode

`R2(config)#exit`	Returns to privileged mode
`R2#copy running-config startup-config`	Saves configuration in NVRAM

R3 Router

`Router>enable`	Moves to privileged mode
`Router#configure terminal`	Moves to global configuration mode
`Router(config)#hostname R3`	Assigns hostname to router
`R3(config)#ip cef`	Enables CEF on device (enabled by default)
`R3(config)#mpls ip`	Enables MPLS globally on device (enabled by default)
`R3(config)#interface loopback 0`	Moves to interface configuration mode
`R3(config-if)#ip address 172.16.3.1 255.255.255.0`	Assigns IP address and netmask
`R3(config-if)#interface serial 0/0/0`	Moves to interface configuration mode
`R3(config-if)#ip address 172.16.20.6 255.255.255.252`	Assigns IP address and netmask
`R3(config-if)#mpls ip`	Enables MPLS on this interface
`R3(config-if)#no shutdown`	Activates interface
`R3(config-if)#exit`	Returns to global configuration mode
`R3(config)#router eigrp 1`	Enables the EIGRP routing process for AS 1
`R3(config-router)#network 172.16.0.0`	Specifies which network to advertise in EIGRP

R3(config-router)#**no auto-summary**	Turns off the auto-summarization feature
R3(config-router)#**exit**	Returns to global configuration mode
R3(config)#**exit**	Returns to privileged mode
R3#**copy running-config startup-config**	Saves configuration in NVRAM

CHAPTER 4

IPsec VPNs

This chapter provides information and commands concerning the following topics:

- Configuring a teleworker to branch office VPN using CLI
- Configuring IPsec site-to-site VPNs using CLI
- Configuring IPsec site-to-site VPNs using SDM
- Configuring GRE tunnels over IPsec
- Configuring a static IPsec virtual tunnel interface
- Configuring High Availability VPNs
  — IPsec backup peers
  — Hot Standby Routing Protocol (HSRP)
  — IPsec stateful failover
  — Backing Up WAN connections with IPsec VPNs
- Configuring Easy VPN Server using Cisco SDM
- Implementing the Cisco VPN Client

Much of this chapter references the network topology shown in Figure 4-1. The Winnipeg and Edmonton routers have a basic configuration to which additional programming will be added.

Figure 4-1   VPN Network Topology

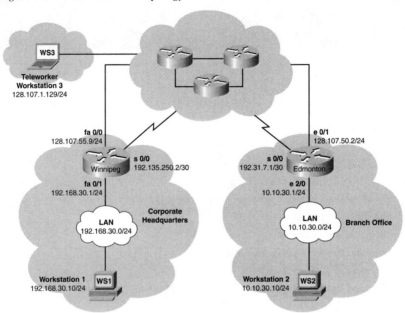

Configuring a Teleworker to Branch Office VPN Using CLI

This section refers to Figure 4-1 and provides details about the configuration for the Edmonton router.

The following steps are used to configure the Edmonton router:

Step 1.   Configure the Internet Security Association and Key Management Protocol (ISAKMP) policy (IKE phase 1).

Step 2.   Configure policies for the client group(s).

Step 3.   Configure the IPsec transform sets (IKE phase 2).

Step 4.   Configure router AAA and add VPN client users.

Step 5.   Create VPN client policy for security association negotiation.

Step 6.   Configure the crypto map.

Step 7.   Apply the crypto map to the interface.

Step 8.   Verify the VPN service.

Step 1: Configure the ISAKMP Policy (IKE Phase 1)

Edmonton(config)#**crypto isakmp policy 1**	Creates an IKE phase 1 policy
Edmonton(config-isakmp)#**encryption 3des**	Selects 3DES as the encryption type
Edmonton(config-isakmp)#**hash md5**	Selects MD5 as the hashing algorithm
Edmonton(config-isakmp)#**authentication pre-share**	Uses a preshared encryption key
Edmonton(config-isakmp)#**group 2**	Uses Diffie-Hellman group 2 key exchange algorithm
Edmonton(config-isakmp)#**exit**	Exits isakmp mode and returns to global configuration mode

Step 2: Configure Policies for the Client Group(s)

Client Group(s)	
Edmonton(config)#**crypto isakmp client configuration group VPNGROUP**	Creates a group for VPN clients
Edmonton(config-isakmp-group)#**key 12345678**	Uses the key 12345678
Edmonton(config-isakmp-group)#**pool VPNPOOL**	Uses addresses defined in the address pool VPNPOOL
Edmonton(config-isakmp-group)#**dns 192.31.7.1**	Points the VPN client to a DNS service
Edmonton(config-isakmp-group)#**wins 10.10.30.10**	Points the VPN client at a WINS service
Edmonton(config-isakmp-group)#**exit**	Exits isakmp-group mode and returns to global configuration mode

Step 3: Configure the IPsec Transform Sets (IKE Phase 2, Tunnel Termination)

Edmonton(config)#**crypto ipsec transform-set TRANSFORM-1 esp-3des esp-sha-hmac**	Creates a transform set for the IKE phase 2 policy
Edmonton(cfg-crypto-trans)#**exit**	Exits cfg-crypto-trans mode

Step 4: Configure Router AAA and Add VPN Client Users

Edmonton(config)#**aaa new-model**	Starts the router AAA service **NOTE:** Cisco IOS–based VPNs require the router AAA service to be enabled. VPN client users can be defined locally in the router or on an AAA server. There are separate lists for authentication and authorization of VPN users.
Edmonton(config)#**aaa authentication login default local**	Verifies login authentication for the "default" group using the local user database
Edmonton(config)#**aaa authentication login VPNAUTH local**	Verifies login authentication for the VPNAUTH group using the local user database
Edmonton(config)#**aaa authorization exec default local**	Verifies EXEC authorization for the "default" group using the local user database
Edmonton(config)#**aaa authorization network VPNAUTHOR local**	Verifies network access authorization for the VPNAUTHOR group using the local user database

`Edmonton(config)#`**`username user1 secret`** **`password1`**	Creates user for VPN authentication
`Edmonton(config)#`**`username user2 secret`** **`password2`**	Creates user for VPN authentication

Step 5: Create VPN Client Policy for Security Association Negotiation

`Edmonton(config)#`**`crypto dynamic-map DYNMAP 1`**	Creates a dynamic crypto map
`Edmonton(config-crypto-map)#`**`set transform-set`** **`TRANSFORM-1`**	Defines the transform set the client must match to
`Edmonton(config-crypto-map)#`**`reverse-route`**	Has the router add a return route for the VPN client in the routing table
`Edmonton(config-crypto-map)#`**`exit`**	Exits config-crypto-map mode

Step 6: Configure the Crypto Map (IKE Phase 2)

`Edmonton(config)#`**`crypto map CRYPTOMAP client`** **`authentication list VPNAUTH`**	Configures IKE extended authentication (Xauth) for the VPN group VPNAUTH
`Edmonton(config)#`**`crypto map CRYPTOMAP isakmp`** **`authorization list VPNAUTHOR`**	Configures IKE key lookup from a AAA server for the VPN group VPNAUTHOR
`Edmonton(config)#`**`crypto map CRYPTOMAP client`** **`configuration address respond`**	Enables the router to accept IP address requests from any peer
`Edmonton(config)#`**`crypto map CRYPTOMAP 65535`** **`ipsec-isakmp dynamic DYNMAP`**	Uses IKE to establish IPsec SAs as specified by crypto map DYNMAP

Step 7: Apply the Crypto Map to the Interface

`Edmonton(config)#interface ethernet 2/0`	Enters interface configuration mode
`Edmonton(config-if)#crypto map CRYPTOMAP`	Applies the crypto map CRYPTOMAP
`Edmonton(config-if)#end`	Exits to privileged mode

Step 8: Verify the VPN Service

`Edmonton#show crypto ipsec sa`	Displays the settings used by current security associations (SA)
`Edmonton#show crypto isakmp sa`	Displays current IKE SAs
`Edmonton#show crypto session`	Displays status information for active crypto sessions
`Edmonton#show crypto dynamic-map`	Displays a dynamic crypto map set
`Edmonton#show crypto map`	Displays the crypto map configuration **NOTE:** Before issuing a **debug** command, you should read the information for that command in the *Cisco IOS Debug Command Reference* for your IOS version to determine the impact on the device.
`Edmonton#debug crypto ipsec`	Displays IPsec
`Edmonton#debug crypto isakmp`	Displays messages about IKE events

Edmonton#**debug crypto isakmp error**	Displays error messages for IKE-related operations
Edmonton#**debug crypto ipsec error**	Displays error messages for IPsec-related operations

Configuring IPsec Site-to-Site VPNs Using CLI

This section refers to Figure 4-1 and provides details about the configuration for the Winnipeg router.

The programming steps for configuring the Winnipeg router are as follows:

Step 1.   Configure the ISAKMP policy (IKE phase 1).

Step 2.   Configure the IPsec transform sets (IKE phase 2, tunnel termination).

Step 3.   Configure the crypto ACL (interesting traffic, secure data transfer).

Step 4.   Configure the crypto map (IKE phase 2).

Step 5.   Apply the crypto map to the interface (IKE phase 2).

Step 6.   Configure the firewall interface ACL.

Step 7.   Verify the VPN service.

Step 1: Configure the ISAKMP Policy (IKE Phase 1)

Winnipeg(config)#**crypto isakmp policy 1**	Creates an IKE policy
Winnipeg(config-isakmp)#**encryption 3des**	Defines 3DES encryption
Winnipeg(config-isakmp)#**hash sha**	Chooses sha as the hashing algorithm
Winnipeg(config-isakmp)#**authentication pre-share**	Specifies authentication with a preshared key
Winnipeg(config-isakmp)#**group 2**	Specifies Diffie-Hellman group 2 key exchange algorithm
Winnipeg(config-isakmp)#**lifetime 86400**	Specifies the lifetime of the IKE SA

`Winnipeg(config-isakmp)#`**`exit`**	Exits isakmp configuration mode
`Winnipeg(config)#`**`crypto isakmp key 12345678`** **`address 192.31.7.1`**	Specifies the key required for the tunnel endpoint **NOTE:** The VPN tunnel peer (Edmonton router) must have one IKE phase 1 policy that matches the IKE phase 1 policy in the Winnipeg router.

Step 2: Configure the IPsec Transform Sets (IKE Phase 2, Tunnel Termination)

`Winnipeg(config)#`**`crypto ipsec transform-set`** **`TRANSFORM-0 esp-sha-hmac esp-3des`**	Creates a transform set for the IKE phase 2 policy
`Winnipeg(cfg-crypto-trans)#`**`mode tunnel`**	Encapsulates the entire datagram
`Winnipeg(cfg-crypto-trans)#`**`exit`**	Exits cfg-crypto-trans mode
`Winnipeg(config)#`**`crypto ipsec security-`** **`association lifetime seconds 1200`**	Defines a 20-minute SA lifetime

Step 3: Configure the Crypto ACL (Interesting Traffic, Secure Data Transfer)

`Winnipeg#`**`configure terminal`**	Enters global configuration mode
`Winnipeg(config)#`**`access-list 100 permit ip`** **`192.168.30.0 0.0.0.255 10.10.30.0 0.0.0.255`**	Defines the source and destination of traffic that will use the IPsec tunnel

Step 4: Configure the Crypto Map (IKE Phase 2)

`Winnipeg(config)#`**`crypto map CRYPTO-MAP-0 1`** **`ipsec-isakmp`**	Defines the crypto map CRYPTO-MAP-0 to use IPsec with ISAKMP
`Winnipeg(config-crypto-map)#`**`set peer`** **`192.31.7.1`**	Specifies the IP address of the VPN peer
`Winnipeg(config-crypto-map)#`**`set transform-set`** **`TRANSFORM-0`**	Uses the transform set TRANSFORM-0 for IKE phase 2 policy
`Winnipeg(config-crypto-map)#`**`match address 100`**	Defines the IP addresses for the IPsec tunnel
`Winnipeg(config-crypto-map)#`**`exit`**	Exits crypto-map configuration mode

NOTE: The Edmonton tunnel termination router has the following mirrored programming: tunnel peer IP address, interesting traffic ACL, and firewall ACL permitting VPN protocols.

`Edmonton(config)#`**`access-list 101 permit ip`** **`10.10.30.0 0.0.0.255 192.168.30.1 0.0.0.255`**	Defines the source and destination IP addresses of the VPN traffic
`Edmonton(config-crypto-map)#`**`match address 101`**	Defines the IP addresses for the IPsec tunnel
`Edmonton(config-crypto-map)#`**`set peer`** **`128.107.55.9`**	Specifies the IP address of the IPsec peer
`Edmonton(config)#`**`access-list 120 permit ahp`** **`host 128.107.55.9 host 192.31.7.1`**	Permits VPN protocol: Authentication Header (AH)
`Edmonton(config)#`**`access-list 120 permit esp`** **`host 128.107.55.9 host 192.31.7.1`**	Permits VPN protocol: Encapsulating Security Payload (ESP)
`Edmonton(config)#`**`access-list 120 permit udp`** **`host 128.107.55.9 host 192.31.7.1 eq isakmp`**	Permits VPN protocol: ISAKMP

Step 5: Apply the Crypto Map to the Interface (IKE Phase 2)

`Winnipeg(config)#interface fastethernet 0/0`	Enters interface configuration mode
`Winnipeg(config-if)#crypto map CRYPTO-MAP-0`	Applies the crypto map at the terminating interface
`Winnipeg(config-if)#exit`	Exits interface configuration mode

Step 6: Configure the Firewall Interface ACL

`Winnipeg(config)#access-list 120 permit ahp host 192.31.7.1 host 128.107.55.9`	Permits VPN protocol: AH
`Winnipeg(config)#access-list 120 permit esp host 192.31.7.1 host 128.107.55.9`	Permits VPN protocol: ESP
`Winnipeg(config)#access-list 120 permit udp host 192.31.7.1 host 128.107.55.9 eq isakmp`	Permits VPN protocol: ISAKMP **NOTE:** The ACL permitting VPN protocols is applied inbound at the border router or firewall WAN interface.
`Winnipeg(config)#interface fastethernet 0/0`	Enters interface configuration mode
`Winnipeg(config-if)#ip access-group 120 in`	Applies VPN protocol ACL inbound at the local terminating interface

Step 7: Verify the VPN Service

`Winnipeg#show crypto ipsec sa`	Displays the settings used by current SAs
`Winnipeg#show crypto isakmp sa`	Displays current IKE SAs
`Winnipeg#show crypto session`	Displays status information for active crypto sessions

`Winnipeg#`**`show crypto dynamic-map`**	Displays a dynamic crypto map set
`Winnipeg#`**`show crypto map`**	Displays the crypto map configuration
`Winnipeg#`**`debug crypto ipsec`**	Displays IPsec events
`Winnipeg#`**`debug crypto isakmp`**	Displays messages about IKE events
`Winnipeg#`**`debug crypto isakmp error`**	Displays error messages for IKE-related operations
`Winnipeg#`**`debug crypto ipsec error`**	Displays error messages for IPsec-related operations

Configuring IPsec Site-to-Site VPNs Using SDM

Figure 4-1 shows the network topology for the configurations that follow, which describe how to use SDM to configure an IPsec site-to-site VPN.

Step 1. Start the Cisco Security Device Manager (SDM) application on a workstation (WorkStation 1) on the 192.168.30.0/24 Winnipeg LAN segment.

Step 2. Choose **Configure > VPN > Tasks > Site-to-Site VPN**.

Step 3. Click the **Create a Site to Site VPN** radio button and then click the **Launch the Selected Task** button.

Step 4. Click the **View Defaults** button and peruse the SDM default crypto selections:

SDM Crypto/IPsec Default Values:

- Authentication Method: Pre-Shared Key
- Encryption: 3DES
- Negotiation Authentication: SHA (Hash)
- Public Key Cryptography: Diffie-Hellman Group 2

Step 5. Click **Next** to display the window shown in Figure 4-2.

Figure 4-2 *Site-to-Site VPN Connection Information*

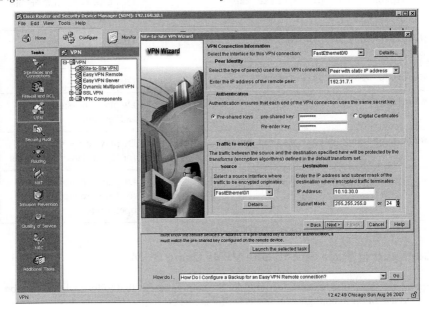

Step 6. In the VPN Connection Information area, click the drop-down arrow and choose **FastEthernet0/0**. FastEthernet 0/0 is the terminating interface on the Winnipeg router.

Step 7. In the Peer Identity area, click the drop-down arrow and choose **Peer with a Static Address**. Enter the IP address (192.31.7.1) of the Edmonton Serial 0/0 interface, which is the terminating interface on the Edmonton router.

Step 8. In the Authentication area, click the **Pre-shared Keys** radio button.

Step 9. In the Source area, enter the source of the VPN traffic. In this case, VPN traffic originates from FastEthernet 0/1 on the Winnipeg router.

Step 10. In the Destination area, enter the destination of the VPN traffic. In this case, the destination of Winnipeg VPN traffic on the Edmonton router is 10.10.30.0/24.

Step 11. Choose **Next > Next** to complete and implement the programming.

NOTE: The Generate Mirror button at the bottom of the page creates a configuration for the peer VPN router. This configuration is only a guide and should *not* be applied directly to the peer VPN router.

NOTE: The IKE policy and preshared keys must be the same on both routers. The ACL applied in the crypto map of each router permits traffic from each local LAN segment to each VPN peer LAN segment.

Step 12. To begin IPsec tunnel troubleshooting, from the window shown in Figure 4-3, click the **Test Tunnel** button and then click **Start**.

NOTE: SDM will attempt to activate the VPN tunnel. It will prompt for a destination host IP in the peer router's internal network and then generate traffic to that peer. SDM will generate an error report with suggested remedies if a tunnel error is encountered.

Step 13. Choose **Monitor > VPN Status > IPsec Tunnels**.

NOTE: Each VPN tunnel configured on the router can be monitored for throughput and errors.

Figure 4-3   SDM Monitoring IPsec Site-to-Site Tunnel

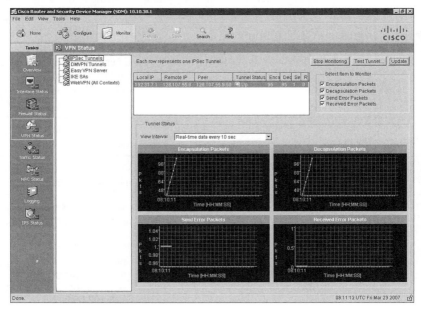

Configuring GRE Tunnels over IPsec

This section refers to Figure 4-1 and provides details about the configuration of a GRE over IPsec tunnel, in this case from Winnipeg to Edmonton.

The programming steps for configuring the Winnipeg router are as follows:

Step 1.   Create the GRE tunnel.

Step 2.   Specify the IPsec VPN authentication method.

Step 3.   Specify the IPsec VPN IKE proposals.

Step 4.   Specify the IPsec VPN transform sets.

Step 5a.   Specify static routing for the GRE over IPsec tunnel.

Step 5b.   Specify routing with OSPF for the GRE over IPsec tunnel.

Step 6.   Enable the crypto programming at the interfaces.

> **NOTE:**   The Winnipeg and Edmonton routers are programmed to provide connectivity for LAN and WAN, including any public to private IP translation.

Step 1: Create the GRE Tunnel

`Winnipeg(config)#interface tunnel0`	Enters interface configuration mode (virtual GRE tunnel interface)
`Winnipeg(config-if)#ip address 192.168.3.1 255.255.255.0`	Assigns the tunnel IP address and netmask
`Winnipeg(config-if)#tunnel source fastethernet 0/0`	Defines the local tunnel interface
`Winnipeg(config-if)#tunnel destination 192.31.7.1`	Programs the far-end tunnel IP **NOTE:** The peer termination router has mirrored programming with "tunnel destination 128.107.55.9."
`Winnipeg(config-if)#no shutdown`	Turns on the tunnel interface

Step 2: Specify the IPsec VPN Authentication Method

`Winnipeg#`**`configure terminal`**	Enters global configuration mode
`Winnipeg(config)#`**`crypto isakmp policy 10`**	Creates an IKE phase 1 policy
`Winnipeg(config-isakmp)#`**`authentication pre-share`**	Specifies use of a preshared encryption key
`Winnipeg(config-isakmp)#`**`encryption 3des`**	Specifies use of 3DES encryption
`Winnipeg(config-isakmp)#`**`group 2`**	Specifies use of the Diffie-Hellman group 2 hashing algorithm
`Winnipeg(config-isakmp)#`**`exit`**	Exits isakmp configuration mode
`Winnipeg(config)#`**`crypto isakmp key 12345678 address 192.31.7.1`**	Specifies the key required for the tunnel endpoint
`Edmonton(config)#`**`crypto isakmp key 12345678 address 128.107.55.9`**	Specifies the key required for the tunnel endpoint **NOTE:** The peer termination router must have the same key and IP address of its peer termination router (128.107.55.9).

Step 3: Specify the IPsec VPN IKE Proposals

`Winnipeg(config)#`**`access-list 101 permit gre host 128.107.55.9 host 192.31.7.1`**	Allows GRE protocol traffic between GRE tunnel endpoints
`Winnipeg(config)#`**`crypto map VPN-1 10 ipsec-isakmp`**	Defines the crypto map VPN-1 to use IPsec with ISAKMP
`Winnipeg(config-crypto-map)#`**`set peer 192.31.7.1`**	Specifies the IP address of the IPsec peer

`Winnipeg(config-crypto-map)#set transform-set` `TO-EDMONTON`	Uses the transform set TO-EDMONTON for IKE phase 2 policy
`Winnipeg(config-crypto-map)#match address 101`	Defines the IP addresses for the IPsec tunnel
`Winnipeg(config-crypto-map)#exit`	Exits crypto-map configuration mode
`Edmonton(config)#access-list 102 permit gre` `host 192.31.7.1 host 128.107.55.9`	Allows GRE protocol traffic between GRE tunnel endpoints
`Edmonton(config-crypto-map)#set peer` `128.107.55.9`	Specifies the IP address of the IPsec peer
`Edmonton(config-crypto-map)#match address 102`	Defines the IP addresses for the IPsec tunnel **NOTE:** The Edmonton tunnel termination router has the following mirrored programming: ACL permitting GRE inbound from the Winnipeg router, tunnel peer, and interesting traffic ACL.

Step 4: Specify the IPsec VPN Transform Sets

`Winnipeg(config)#crypto ipsec transform-set` `TO-EDMONTON esp-des esp-md5-hmac`	Creates the transform set TO-EDMONTON for the IKE phase 2 policy
`Winnipeg(cfg-crypto-trans)#exit`	Exits cfg-crypto-trans configuration mode

Step 5a: Specify Static Routing for the GRE over IPsec Tunnel

`Winnipeg(config)#`**`ip route 0.0.0.0 0.0.0.0`** **`128.107.55.10`**	Configures a static default route to the physical next-hop IP address
`Winnipeg(config)#`**`ip route 10.10.30.0`** **`255.255.255.0 192.168.3.2`**	Configures a static route for (local) tunnel traffic giving the far-end tunnel address as the next-hop IP address

Step 5b: Specify Routing with OSPF for the GRE over IPsec Tunnel

`Winnipeg(config)#`**`router ospf 1`**	Enables OSPF with process ID 1
`Winnipeg(config-router)#`**`passive-interface`** **`fastethernet 0/0`**	Disables OSPF routing updates on interface FastEthernet 0/0
`Winnipeg(config-router)#`**`passive-interface`** **`fastethernet 0/1`**	Disables OSPF routing updates on interface FastEthernet 0/1 **NOTE:** Interface Tunnel0 is the only interface participating in OSPF.
`Winnipeg(config-router)#`**`network 192.168.30.0`** **`0.0.0.255 area 0`**	Configures 192.168.30.0/24 into OSPF area 0
`Winnipeg(config-router)#`**`network 192.168.3.0`** **`0.0.0.255 area 0`**	Any interface with an address of 192.168.3.x is to be placed into area 0
`Winnipeg(config-router)#`**`exit`**	Returns to global configuration mode

NOTE: GRE is multiprotocol and can tunnel any OSI Layer 3 protocol.

Step 6: Enable the Crypto Programming at the Interfaces

`Winnipeg(config-if)#`**`interface fastethernet 0/0`**	Enters interface configuration mode
`Winnipeg(config-if)#`**`shutdown`**	Turns the interface off
`Winnipeg(config-if)#`**`crypto map VPN-1`**	Applies the crypto map to the WAN interface
`Winnipeg(config-if)#`**`no shutdown`**	Turns the interface on
`Winnipeg(config-if)#`**`exit`**	Returns to global configuration mode
`Winnipeg(config)#`**`interface tunnel0`**	Enters interface configuration mode
`Winnipeg(config-if)#`**`shutdown`**	Turns the interface off
`Winnipeg(config-if)#`**`crypto map VPN-1`**	Applies the crypto map to the tunnel interface
`Winnipeg(config-if)#`**`no shutdown`**	Turns the interface on

Configuring a Static IPsec Virtual Tunnel Interface

This section refers to Figure 4-1 and provides details about the configuration of an IPsec virtual tunnel interface (VTI).

> **NOTE:** The VTI method to secure multiprotocol links is preferred over secure GRE tunnels. IPsec VTIs simplify the configuration of IPsec for protection of remote links. This feature may not be supported in older IOS releases. Please review the VTI restrictions in *Cisco IOS Security Configuration Guide, Release 12.4,* "Part 4: Implementing IPsec and IKE" (click the **Configuring Security for VPNs with IPsec** link and then click **IPsec Virtual Tunnel Interface**) at Cisco.com.

The programming steps for configuring a router (for this example, the Winnipeg and Edmonton routers) for a static IPsec VTI are as follows:

Step 1. Configure EIGRP AS 1.

Step 2. Configure Static Routing.

Step 3. Create IKE Policies and Peers.

Step 4.   Create IPsec Transform Sets.

Step 5.   Create an IPsec Profile.

Step 6.   Create the IPsec Virtual Tunnel Interface.

Step 1: Configure EIGRP AS 1

Winnipeg(config)#**router eigrp 1**	Enters EIGRP routing configuration mode
Winnipeg(config-router)#**no auto-summary**	Turns off EIGRP's address summarization
Winnipeg(config-router)#**network 192.168.3.0**	Advertises the IP segment on the tunnel interface
Winnipeg(config-router)#**network 192.168.30.0**	Advertises the LAN IP segment
Edmonton(config)#**router eigrp 1**	Enters EIGRP routing configuration mode
Edmonton(config-router)#**no auto-summary**	Turns off EIGRP's address summarization
Edmonton(config-router)#**network 192.168.3.0**	Advertises the IP segment on the tunnel interface
Edmonton(config-router)#**network 10.10.30.0**	Advertises the LAN IP segment

Step 2: Configure Static Routing

Winnipeg(config)#**ip route 0.0.0.0 0.0.0.0 128.107.55.10**	Specifies default route to next-hop WAN address
Edmonton(config)#**ip route 0.0.0.0 0.0.0.0 192.31.7.2**	Specifies default route to next-hop WAN address **NOTE:** After Steps 1 through 3, connectivity and EIGRP neighbor relationships should be verified.

Step 3: Create IKE Policies and Peers

`Winnipeg(config)#`**`crypto isakmp policy 10`**	Creates a policy to define the parameters used during the IKE negotiation. **NOTE:** All ISAKMP settings are not offered on all crypto-capable IOS images. Configure the settings supported by your IOS image.
`Winnipeg(config-isakmp)#`**`authentication pre-share`**	Specifies use of a shared common key
`Winnipeg(config-isakmp)#`**`encryption aes 256`**	Specifies use of 256-bit AES encryption
`Winnipeg(config-isakmp)#`**`hash sha`**	Specifies use of the SHA hashing algorithm
`Winnipeg(config-isakmp)#`**`group 5`**	Configures the IKE policy with the 1536-bit Diffie-Hellman group (group 5)
`Winnipeg(config-isakmp)#`**`lifetime 3600`**	Specifies the lifetime of an IKE SA **NOTE:** The IKE SA is bound to the VTI. Because the IKE SA is bound to the VTI, the same IKE SA cannot be used for a crypto map.
`Winnipeg(config)#`**`exit`**	Returns to global configuration mode

Winnipeg(config)#**crypto isakmp key KEY-1 address 0.0.0.0 0.0.0.0**	Assigns the common crypto key and specifies the interface IP address of the participating peer **NOTE:** The VTI programming steps for the Edmonton router are the same as those for the Winnipeg router using reciprocal (mirrored) addressing.
Edmonton(config)#**crypto isakmp policy 10**	Creates policy to define the parameters used during the IKE negotiation
Edmonton(config-isakmp)#**authentication pre-share**	Specifies use of a shared common key
Edmonton(config-isakmp)#**encryption aes 256**	Specifies use of 256-bit AES encryption
Edmonton(config-isakmp)#**hash sha**	Specifies use of the SHA hashing algorithm
Edmonton(config-isakmp)#**group 5**	Configures the IKE policy with the 1536-bit Diffie-Hellman group (group 5)
Edmonton(config-isakmp)#**lifetime 3600**	Specifies the lifetime of an IKE SA
Edmonton(config)#**exit**	Returns to global configuration mode
Edmonton(config)#**crypto isakmp key KEY-1 address 0.0.0.0 0.0.0.0**	Assigns the common crypto key and specifies the interface IP address of the participating peer

Step 4: Create IPsec Transform Sets

> **NOTE:** When IKE is not used to establish SAs, a single transform set must be used. The transform set is not negotiated, and the IPsec transform set must be configured in tunnel mode only.

`Winnipeg(config)#`**`crypto ipsec transform-set`** **`TRANSFORM-1 esp-aes 256 esp-sha-hmac ah-sha-`** **`hmac`**	Specifies the IPsec security protocol (AH or ESP) and the algorithm you want to use
`Winnipeg(cfg-crypto-trans)#`**`exit`**	Returns to global configuration mode
`Winnipeg(config)#`	**NOTE:** All IPsec transform settings are not offered on all crypto-capable IOS images. Configure the settings supported by your IOS image.
`Edmonton(config)#`**`crypto ipsec transform-set`** **`TRANSFORM-1 esp-aes 256 esp-sha-hmac ah-sha-`** **`hmac`**	Specifies the IPsec security protocol (AH or ESP) and the algorithm you want to use
`Edmonton(cfg-crypto-trans)#`**`exit`**	Returns to global configuration mode
`Edmonton(config)#`	

Step 5: Create an IPsec Profile

> **CAUTION:** Static VTIs support only a single IPsec SA that is attached to the VTI interface. The traffic selector for the IPsec SA is always **"IP any any"**.

`Winnipeg(config)#`**`crypto ipsec profile`** `PROFILE-1`	Creates the Winnipeg IPsec profile PROFILE-1
`Winnipeg(ipsec-profile)#`**`set transform-set`** `TRANSFORM-1`	Links the transform TRANSFORM-1 to the profile PROFILE-1 **NOTE:** There are no **match** clauses in an IPsec profile, only set statements. Also, the *transform set* is the only parameter that *must* be defined under the profile.
`Edmonton(config)#`**`crypto ipsec profile`** `PROFILE-1`	Creates the Edmonton IPsec profile PROFILE-1 on the Edmonton router
`Edmonton(ipsec-profile)#`**`set transform-set`** `TRANSFORM-1`	Links the transform TRANSFORM-1 to the profile PROFILE-1

Step 6: Create the IPsec Virtual Tunnel Interface

`Winnipeg(config)#`**`interface tunnel 0`**	Creates a "tunnel" interface
`Winnipeg(config-if)#`**`ip address 192.168.3.1 255.255.255.0`**	Assigns the tunnel IP address
`Winnipeg(config-if)#`**`tunnel source fastethernet 0/0`**	Declares the local physical interface used by the tunnel interface
`Winnipeg(config-if)#`**`tunnel destination 128.107.50.2`**	Names the IP address of the remote tunnel endpoint
`Winnipeg(config-if)#`**`tunnel mode ipsec ipv4`**	Sets IPsec using IPv4 as the encapsulation mode for the tunnel interface
`Winnipeg(config-if)#`**`tunnel protection ipsec profile PROFILE-1`**	Associates the tunnel interface with the IPsec profile

`Edmonton(config)#`**`interface tunnel 0`**	Creates a tunnel interface
`Edmonton(config-if)#`**`ip address 192.168.3.2`** **`255.255.255.0`**	Assigns the tunnel IP address and netmask
`Edmonton(config-if)#`**`tunnel source ethernet 0/1`**	Declares the local physical interface used by the tunnel interface
`Edmonton(config-if)#`**`tunnel destination`** **`128.107.55.9`**	Names the IP address of the remote tunnel endpoint
`Edmonton(config-if)#`**`tunnel mode ipsec ipv4`**	Sets IPsec using IPv4 as the encapsulation mode for the tunnel interface
`Edmonton(config-if)#`**`tunnel protection ipsec`** **`profile PROFILE-1`**	Associates the tunnel interface with the IPsec profile

Configuring High Availability VPNs

Figure 4-4 shows the network topology for IPSec stateful failover using the Hot Standby Router Protocol (HSRP).

Figure 4-4   HSRP Stateful Failover

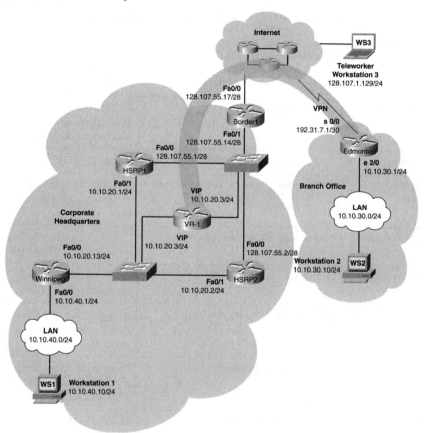

The programming steps for configuring a router (for this example, the HSRP1 and HSRP2 routers) for IPsec HRSP stateful failover are as follows:

Step 1.   Configure Hot Standby Router Protocol on HSRP1.

Step 2.   Configure site-to-site VPN on HSRP1.

Step 3.   Add programming for crypto redundancy configuration.

Step 4.   Define the interdevice communication protocol (HSRP1 and HSRP).

Step 5.   Apply the programming at the interface.

NOTE: There are design restrictions when configuring stateful redundancy for VPN connections. These encompass platform, IOS compatibility, and connection topology.

Step 1: Configure Hot Standby Routing Protocol Configuration on HSRP1

`HSRP1(config)#`**`interface fastethernet 0/0`**	Enters interface configuration mode
`HSRP1(config-if)#`**`standby 1 ip 128.107.55.3`**	Assigns 128.107.55.3 as the HSRP group 1 virtual router IP
`HSRP1(config-if)#`**`standby 1 preempt`**	Enables the active device to release control after an interface tracking event
`HSRP1(config-if)#`**`standby 1 name HSRP-OUT`**	Names the HSRP group
`HSRP1(config-if)#`**`standby 1 track fastethernet 1/0`**	Monitors the interface status to enable failover to an HSRP peer
`HSRP1(config-if)#`**`standby delay reload 120`**	Configures a delay before initializing HSRP groups
`HSRP1(config)#`**`interface fastethernet 0/1`**	Enters interface configuration mode
`HSRP1(config-if)#`**`standby 2 ip 10.10.20.3`**	Assigns s10.10.20.3 as the HSRP group 2 virtual router IP
`HSRP1(config-if)#`**`standby 2 preempt`**	Enables the active device to release control after an interface tracking event
`HSRP1(config-if)#`**`standby 2 name HSRP-IN`**	Names the HSRP group
`HSRP1(config-if)#`**`standby delay reload 120`**	Configures a delay before initializing HSRP groups
`HSRP1(config-if)#`**`standby 2 track fastethernet 0/0`**	Monitors the interface status to enable failover to an HSRP peer
`HSRP2(config)#`**`interface fastethernet 0/0`**	Enters interface configuration mode

HSRP2(config-if)#**standby 1 ip 128.107.55.3**	Assigns 128.107.55.3 as the HSRP group 1 virtual router IP
HSRP2(config-if)#**standby 1 preempt**	Enables the active device to release control after an interface tracking event
HSRP2(config-if)#**standby 1 name HSRP-OUT**	Names the HSRP group
HSRP2(config-if)#**standby 1 track fastethernet 1/0**	Monitors the interface status to enable failover to an HSRP peer
HSRP2(config-if)#**standby delay reload 120**	Configures a delay before initializing HSRP groups
HSRP2(config)#**interface fastethernet 0/1**	Enters interface configuration mode
HSRP2(config-if)#**standby 2 ip 10.10.20.3**	Assigns 10.10.20.3 as the HSRP group 2 virtual router IP
HSRP2(config-if)#**standby 2 preempt**	Enables the active device to release control after an interface tracking event
HSRP2(config-if)#**standby 2 name HSRP-IN**	Names the HSRP group
HSRP2(config-if)#**standby delay reload 120**	Configures a delay before initializing HSRP groups
HSRP2(config-if)#**standby 2 track fastethernet 0/0**	Monitors the interface status to enable failover to an HSRP peer

Step 2: Configure Site-to-Site VPN on HSRP1

HSRP1 Configuration

Tunnel Traffic Filter

HSRP1(config)#**ip access-list extended PEER-OUTSIDE**	Creates a named extended access list
HSRP1(config-ext-nacl)#**permit ip 10.10.40.1 0.0.0.255 10.10.30.0 0.0.0.255**	Defines traffic for the IPsec tunnel
HSRP1(config-ext-nacl)#**exit**	Exits to global configuration mode

Key Exchange Policy

HSRP1(config)#**crypto isakmp policy 1**	Creates IKE policy
HSRP1(config-isakmp)#**authentication pre-share**	Specifies use of a preshared key for authentication
HSRP1(config-isakmp)#**exit**	Exits to global configuration mode

Addressing, Authentication Credentials, and Transform Set

HSRP1(config)#**crypto isakmp key 12345678 address 0.0.0.0 0.0.0.0 no-xauth**	Specifies the key required for the tunnel endpoint (no user authentication)
HSRP1(config)#**crypto ipsec transform-set TRANS-1 ah-md5-hmac esp-3des**	Creates the transform set TRANS-1 for the IKE phase 2 policy
HSRP1(cfg-crypto-trans)#**exit**	Exits to global configuration mode

IPsec Tunnel

HSRP1(config)#**crypto map TO-OUTSIDE 10 ipsec-isakmp**	Defines the crypto map TO-OUTSIDE to use IPsec with ISAKMP
HSRP1(config-crypto-map)#**set peer 192.31.7.1**	Specifies the IP address of the remote IPsec peer
HSRP1(config-crypto-map)#**set transform-set TRANS-1**	Specifies use of the transform set TRANS-1 for IKE phase 2 policy
HSRP1(config-crypto-map)#**match address PEER-OUTSIDE**	Defines the IP addresses for the IPsec tunnel
HSRP1(config-crypto-map)#**exit**	Exits to global configuration mode

HSRP2 Configuration

Tunnel Traffic Filter

`HSRP2(config)#ip access-list extended PEER-` `OUTSIDE`	Creates named extended access list
`HSRP2(config-ext-nacl)#permit ip 10.10.40.1` `0.0.0.255 10.10.30.0 0.0.0.255`	Defines traffic for the IPsec tunnel
`HSRP2(config-ext-nacl)#exit`	Exits to global configuration mode

Key Exchange Policy

`HSRP2(config)#crypto isakmp policy 1`	Creates IKE policy
`HSRP2(config-isakmp)#authentication pre-share`	Specifies the use of a preshared key for authentication
`HSRP2(config-isakmp)#exit`	Exits to global configuration mode

Addressing, Authentication Credentials, and Transform Set

`HSRP2(config)#crypto isakmp key 12345678` `address 0.0.0.0 0.0.0.0 no-xauth`	Specifies the key required for the tunnel endpoint (no user authentication)
`HSRP2(config)#crypto ipsec transform-set` `TRANS-1 ah-md5-hmac esp-3des`	Creates the transform set TRANS-1 for the IKE phase 2 policy
`HSRP2(cfg-crypto-trans)#exit`	Exits to global configuration mode

IPsec Tunnel

`HSRP2(config)#crypto map TO-OUTSIDE 10 ipsec-` `isakmp`	Defines the crypto map VPN-2 to use IPsec with ISAKMP
`HSRP2(config-crypto-map)#set peer 192.31.7.1`	Specifies the IP address of the IPsec peer

`HSRP2(config-crypto-map)#`**`set transform-set`** **`TRANS-1`**	Specifies the use of the transform set TRANS-1 for IKE phase 2 policy
`HSRP2(config-crypto-map)#`**`match address PEER-`** **`OUTSIDE`**	Defines the IP addresses for the IPsec tunnel
`HSRP2(config-crypto-map)#`**`exit`**	Exits to global configuration mode

Step 3: Add Programming for Crypto Redundancy Configuration

`HSRP1(config)#`**`crypto ipsec transform-set`** **`TRANS-2 ah-md5-hmac esp-aes`**	Creates the transform set TRANS-2 for the IKE phase 2 policy
`HSRP1(cfg-crypto-trans)#`**`exit`**	Exits to global configuration mode
`HSRP1(config)#`**`crypto ipsec profile SSO1-SECURE`**	Creates the general profile SSO1-SECURE for IPsec policy
`HSRP1(ipsec-profile)#`**`set transform-set TRANS-2`**	Specifies a transform set
`HSRP1(ipsec-profile)#`**`exit`**	Exits to global configuration mode
`HSRP1(config)#`**`redundancy inter-device`**	Enters interdevice configuration mode
`HSRP1(config-red-interdevice)#`**`scheme standby`** **`HSRP-IN`**	Names the redundancy scheme used between two devices
`HSRP1(config-red-interdevice)#`**`security ipsec`** **`SSO1-SECURE`**	Specifies the IPsec profile
`HSRP1(config-red-interdevice)#`**`exit`**	Exits to global configuration mode
`HSRP2(config)#`**`crypto ipsec profile SSO2-SECURE`**	Creates the general profile SSO1-SECURE for IPsec policy
`HSRP2(ipsec-profile)#`**`set transform-set TRANS-2`**	Specifies a transform set

`HSRP2(ipsec-profile)#`**`exit`**	Exits to global configuration mode
`HSRP2(config)#`**`redundancy inter-device`**	Enters interdevice configuration mode
`HSRP2(config-red-interdevice)#`**`scheme standby HSRP-IN`**	Names the redundancy scheme used between two devices
`HSRP2(config-red-interdevice)#`**`security ipsec SSO2-SECURE`**	Specifies the IPsec profile
`HSRP2(config-red-interdevice)#`**`exit`**	Exits to global configuration mode

Step 4: Define the Interdevice Communication Protocol (HSRP1 and HSRP)

`HSRP1(config)#`**`ipc zone default`**	Configures the interdevice communication protocol
`HSRP1(config-ipczone)#`**`association 1`**	Creates an association between the two devices
`HSRP1(config-ipczone-assoc)#`**`no shutdown`**	Enables the association
`HSRP1(config-ipczone-assoc)#`**`protocol sctp`**	Configures Stream Control Transmission Protocol (SCTP)
`HSRP1(config-ipc-protocol-sctp)#`**`local-port 5000`**	Defines the local SCTP port number used to communicate with the redundant peer
`HSRP1(config-ipc-local-sctp)#`**`local-ip 10.10.20.1`**	Defines a local IP to communicate with the peer
`HSRP1(config-ipc-local-sctp)#`**`exit`**	Exits SCTP local configuration mode
`HSRP1(config-ipc-protocol-sctp)#`**`remote-port 5000`**	Defines the remote SCTP port number used to communicate with the redundant peer

`HSRP1(config-ipc-remote-sctp)#`**`remote-ip`** **`10.10.20.2`**	Defines a remote IP to communicate with the peer
`HSRP1(config-ipc-remote-sctp)#`**`exit`**	Returns to local-ip configuration mode
`HSRP1(config-ipc-protocol-sctp)#`**`exit`**	Returns to config-ipczone-assoc mode
`HSRP1(config-ipczone-assoc)#`**`exit`**	Returns to config-ipczone mode
`HSRP1(config-ipczone)#`**`exit`**	Returns to global configuration mode
`HSRP1(config)#`	
`HSRP2(config)#`**`ipc zone default`**	Configures the interdevice communication protocol
`HSRP2(config-ipczone)#`**`association 1`**	Creates an association between the two devices
`HSRP2(config-ipczone-assoc)#`**`no shutdown`**	Enables the association
`HSRP2(config-ipczone-assoc)#`**`protocol sctp`**	Configures SCTP
`HSRP2(config-ipc-protocol-sctp)#`**`local-port`** **`5000`**	Defines the local SCTP port number used to communicate with the redundant peer
`HSRP2(config-ipc-local-sctp)#`**`local-ip`** **`10.10.20.2`**	Defines a/the local IP to communicate with the peer
`HSRP2(config-ipc-local-sctp)#`**`exit`**	Exits SCTP local configuration mode
`HSRP2(config-ipc-protocol-sctp)#`**`remote-port`** **`5000`**	Defines the remote SCTP port number used to communicate with the redundant peer
`HSRP2(config-ipc-remote-sctp)#`**`remote-ip`** `10.10.20.1`	Defines a remote IP to communicate with the peer

`HSRP2(config-ipc-remote-sctp)#`**`exit`**	Returns to local-ip configuration mode
`HSRP2(config-ipc-protocol-sctp)#`**`exit`**	Returns to config-ipczone-assoc mode
`HSRP2(config-ipczone-assoc)#`**`exit`**	Returns to config-ipczone mode
`HSRP2(config-ipczone)#`**`exit`**	Returns to global configuration mode
`HSRP2(config)#`	

Step 5: Apply the Programming at the Interface

`HSRP1(config)#`**`interface fastethernet 0/0`**	Enters interface configuration mode
`HSRP1(config-if)#`**`crypto map TO-OUTSIDE redundancy HSRP-OUT stateful`**	Applies the crypto map to the WAN-facing interface
`HSRP1(config-if)#`**`end`**	Returns to privileged EXEC mode
`HSRP1#`	
`HSRP2(config)#`**`interface fastethernet 0/0`**	Enters interface configuration mode
`HSRP2(config-if)#`**`crypto map TO-OUTSIDE redundancy HSRP-OUT stateful`**	Applies the crypto map to the WAN-facing interface
`HSRP2(config-if)#`**`end`**	Returns to privileged EXEC mode
`HSRP2#`	

Configuring Easy VPN Server Using Cisco SDM

This section refers to the network topology shown in Figure 4-1 and provides details about the configuration of Easy VPN Server:

Step 1.   Start the Cisco Security Device Manager application at 192.168.30.1, the Winnipeg router LAN segment interface.

Step 2.   Choose **Home > Configure > VPN > Tasks > Easy VPN Server**.

Step 3. Choose **Enable AAA** and click **Yes** in the resulting dialog box, shown in Figure 4-5.

Figure 4-5 Enabling AAA on Easy VPN Server

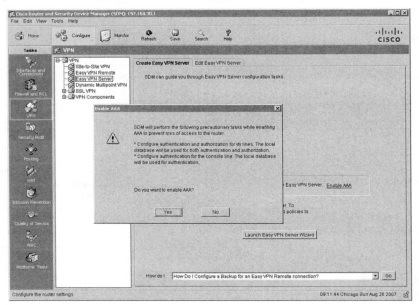

NOTE: One of the prerequisites of remote client authentication for the VPN service is enabling the AAA service on the target router.

Step 4. Click the **Launch Easy VPN Server Wizard** button and then click **Next**.

Step 5. Choose **FastEthernet0/0**. This is the VPN service termination interface.

Step 6. Click the Pre-Shared Keys radio button and then click Next to use preshared keys as the authentication method.

Step 7. Choose the default IKE proposal and click **Next**.

NOTE: The default SDM IKE policy is as follows:
- Authentication Method: Pre-Shared Key
- Encryption: 3DES
- Negotiation Authentication: SHA (Hash)
- Public Key Cryptography: Diffie-Hellman Group 2
- Security Association Lifetime: 1 hour

Step 8.   Select **SDM Default Transform Set > Next**. Use the default encryption and authentication algorithms in the IPsec tunnel.

Step 9.   Choose the **Local** radio button in the Group Authorization and Group Policy window and then click **Next**.

Step 10.   Select **Enable User Authentication** in the User Authentication window and choose the **Local Only** radio button. Click **Next**. The router local user database will be used for authentication with the client policy group.

Step 11.   Click the **Add** button in the Group Authorization and User Group Policy window to create a specific user policy group (see Figure 4-6).

Figure 4-6   *Adding VPN Client Group Policies*

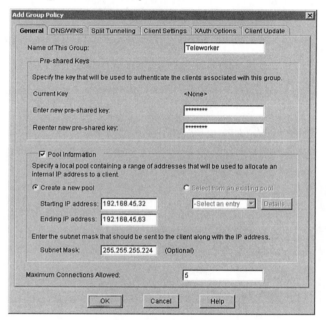

Step 12.   Enter a VPN client-group name and a chosen preshared key.

Step 13.   Check the **Pool Information** check box, click the **Create a New Pool** radio button, and enter the Starting IP Address and Ending IP Address of the VPN client pool.

NOTE: The addresses in the pool are assigned to new VPN clients as they connect. Choose an address range or network that is not already in use and that can be accurately defined by a subnet mask. The addresses chosen do not need to be associated to a physical interface on the router.

CAUTION: Be sure to adjust/edit any ACL in a remote LAN segment or firewalls to accommodate the addresses programmed in any VPN address pool(s).

NOTE: On the DNS/WINS tab, configure any corporate DNS or WINS server addresses that the remote VPN client needs to reference.

Step 14.   Click **OK** and then click **Next** in the Group Authorization and User Group Policies window.

Step 15.   Review and verify the IPsec VPN choices and click **Finish** when completed.

Step 16.   To add user accounts, choose **Configure** > **Additional Tasks**.

Step 17.   In the Additional Tasks pane, choose **Router Access** > **User Accounts/View** and then click the **Add** button to display the window shown in Figure 4-7.

Figure 4-7   Adding VPN User to Router Local Database

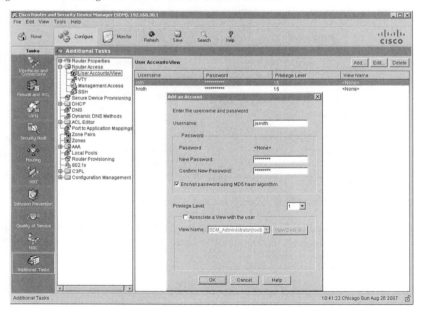

Step 18.   Create VPN client usernames and passwords and assign a privilege level.
Click **OK** to add the user account to the local user database.

NOTE: Accept the default privilege level, 1, unless this user is required to
program the router at the command prompt or through the SDM GUI.

Implementing the Cisco VPN Client

Step 1.   Install and start the Cisco VPN Client application.

Step 2.   Click the **New** connection entry icon.

Step 3.   Complete the fields as shown in Figure 4-8.

NOTE: The Host field is the IP address at the VPN terminating interface of the
router.

NOTE: The Group Authentication Name and Password must coincide with the
Group and Key entries on the router.

Figure 4-8   *Cisco VPN Client Create New VPN Connection Entry Dialog Box*

CHAPTER 5

Cisco Device Hardening

This chapter provides information and commands concerning the following topics:

- Disabling unneeded services and interfaces
- Disabling commonly configured management services
- Disabling path integrity mechanisms
- Disabling features related to probes and scans
- Terminal access security
- Gratuitous and proxy Address Resolution Protocol
- Disabling IP directed broadcasts
- Locking down routers with AutoSecure
- Optional AutoSecure parameters
- Locking down routers with Cisco SDM
- Setting Cisco passwords and password security
- Securing ROMMON
- Setting a login failure rate
- Setting timeouts
- Setting multiple privilege levels
- Configuring banner messages
- Role-Based CLI
- Secure configuration files
- Tips for using Cisco access control lists
- Using ACLs to filter network traffic to mitigate threats
- Mitigating dedicated DoS (DDoS) attacks with ACLs
- Configuring an SSH server for secure management and reporting
- Configuring syslog logging
- Configuring an SNMP managed node
- Configuring NTP clients and servers
- Configuration example: NTP
- Configuring AAA on Cisco routers using CLI
- Configuring AAA on Cisco routers using SDM

Disabling Unneeded Services and Interfaces

`Router(config)#`**`interface serial 0/0/0`**	Moves to interface configuration mode
`Router(config-if)#`**`shutdown`**	Logically disables the interface
`Router(config-if)#`**`exit`**	Returns to global configuration mode
`Router(config)#`**`no ip bootp server`**	Does not permit the router to act as a BOOTP server for other network devices
`Router(config)#`**`no cdp run`**	Do not advertise CDP information globally between Cisco devices.
`Router(config)#`**`interface gigabitethernet 0/1`**	Moves to interface configuration mode
`Router(config-if)#`**`no cdp enable`**	Instructs the router to not advertise CDP information between Cisco devices at the interface level
`Router(config-if)#`**`exit`**	Returns to global configuration mode
`Router(config)#`**`no service config`**	Disables the config service **NOTE:** The config service allows for the autoloading of configuration files from a network server.
`Router(config)#`**`no ftp-server enable`**	Globally disables the router FTP service

Router(config)#**no tftp-server** *file-sys:imagename*	Disables the TFTP service to serve the IOS image at the listed location
Router(config)#**no ntp server** *ip-address*	Disables both NTP server and client capabilities
Router(config)#**no service pad**	Disables X.25 packet assembler/disassembler (PAD) service
Router(config)#**no service tcp-small-servers**	Disables minor TCP services—echo, discard, chargen, and daytime—available from hosts on the network
Router(config)#**no service udp-small-servers**	Disables minor UDP services—echo, discard, chargen, and daytime—available from hosts on the network
Router(config-if)#**no mop enabled**	Disables the Digital Equipment Corporation (DEC) Maintenance Operations Protocol

NOTE: The BOOTP, CDP, and PAD services are enabled by default. Configuration auto-loading, FTP, TFTP, and NTP services are disabled by default. TCP and UDP minor services are enabled by default prior to Cisco IOS Release 11.3 and disabled by default in Cisco IOS Release 11.3 and later. The MOP service is enabled on most Ethernet interfaces.

Disabling Commonly Configured Management Services

`Router(config)#no snmp-server enable`	Disables router response to SNMP queries and configuration requests **NOTE:** If SNMP is required, use SNMPv3 whenever possible. SNMPv3 offers secure communication previously unavailable in earlier versions. If HTTP or HTTPS service is required, use access control lists (ACL) to restrict access.
`Router(config)#no ip http server`	Disables monitoring and configuration from a web browser
`Router(config)#no ip http secure-server`	Disables monitoring and configuration from a secure (HTTPS) web browser
`Router(config)#no ip domain-lookup`	Disables undirected broadcast (255.255.255.255) as the default address to reach a DNS server

NOTE: The **no ip domain-lookup** command also disables all DNS on the system.

Disabling Path Integrity Mechanisms

`Router(config)#no ip icmp redirect`	Prevents the router from sending ICMP redirects
`Router(config)#no ip source-route`	Disables a sender from controlling the route that a packet travels through a network

Disabling Features Related to Probes and Scans

`Router(config)#no service finger`	Disables the retrieval of user information from port 79
`Router(config)#interface gigabitethernet 0/0`	Moves to interface configuration mode
`Router(config-if)#no ip unreachables`	Disables the notification of invalid destination IP subnets or specific addresses
`Router(config-if)#no ip mask-reply`	Disables replies to an ICMP subnet mask query

Terminal Access Security

`Router(config)#no ip identd`	Do not report the identity of a TCP connection initiator.
`Router(config)#service tcp-keepalives-in`	Allows a router to detect when the host with which it is communicating experiences a failure
`Router(config)#service tcp-keepalives-out`	Allows a router to detect when the host with which it is communicating experiences a failure **NOTE:** TCP keepalives are sent once every minute and connection is closed if no keepalives are detected after 5 minutes.

Gratuitous and Proxy Address Resolution Protocol

`Router(config)#no ip gratuitous-arps`	Instructs the router to not generate gratuitous ARPs for PPP/SLIP peer addresses
`Router(config)#interface serial 0/0/1`	Moves to interface configuration mode
`Router(config)#no ip proxy-arp`	Disables proxy ARP on the specified interface

Disabling IP Directed Broadcasts

`Router(config)#interface gigabitethernet 0/0`	Moves to interface configuration mode
`Router(config-if)#no ip directed-broadcast`	Specifies that directed broadcasts destined for the subnet to which that interface is attached will be dropped, rather than being broadcast

Locking Down Routers with AutoSecure

AutoSecure is a single privileged EXEC program that allows you to eliminate many potential security threats quickly and easily. AutoSecure helps to make you more efficient at securing Cisco routers. Cisco AutoSecure is available in Cisco IOS Software Major Release 12.3 and subsequent 12.3 T releases for the Cisco 800, 1700, 2600, 3600, 3700, 7200, and 7500 Series routers.

2821Router#**auto secure**	Enters AutoSecure configuration mode
--- AutoSecure Configuration --- *** AutoSecure configuration enhances the security of the router, but it will not make it absolutely resistant to all security attacks *** AutoSecure will modify the configuration of your device. All configuration changes will be shown. For a detailed explanation of how the configuration changes enhance security and any possible side effects, please refer to Cisco.com for Autosecure documentation. At any prompt you may enter '?' for help. Use ctrl-c to abort this session at any prompt. Gathering information about the router for AutoSecure	
Is this router connected to internet? [no]: **y**	Prompts the user to enter **y** if the device is connected to the Internet
Enter the number of interfaces facing the internet [1]: **1**	Prompts the user to enter the number of interfaces facing the Internet

Interface	IP-Address	OK?	Method	Status	Protocol
GigabitEthernet0/0	192.168.100.1	YES	NVRAM	up	up
GigabitEthernet0/1	192.31.7.1	YES	manual	up	up
FastEthernet0/1/0	unassigned	YES	unset	up	down
FastEthernet0/1/1	unassigned	YES	unset	up	down
FastEthernet0/1/2	unassigned	YES	unset	up	down
FastEthernet0/1/3	unassigned	YES	unset	up	down
FastEthernet0/1/4	unassigned	YES	unset	up	down
FastEthernet0/1/5	unassigned	YES	unset	up	down
FastEthernet0/1/6	unassigned	YES	unset	up	down
FastEthernet0/1/7	unassigned	YES	unset	up	down
FastEthernet0/1/8	unassigned	YES	unset	up	down
Serial0/2/0	unassigned	YES	NVRAM	administratively down	down
Serial0/2/1	unassigned	YES	NVRAM	administratively down	down
Vlan1	unassigned	YES	NVRAM	up	down

Enter the interface name that is facing the internet: **gigabitethernet0/1**	Prompts the user to enter the name of the interface that is facing the Internet.
Securing Management plane services…	Secures the management plane services
Disabling service finger Disabling service pad Disabling udp & tcp small servers Enabling service password encryption Enabling service tcp-keepalives-in Enabling service tcp-keepalives-out Disabling the cdp protocol Disabling the bootp server Disabling the http server Disabling the finger service Disabling source routing Disabling gratuitous arp	

Here is a sample Security Banner to be shown at every access to device. Modify it to suit your
 	
enterprise requirements.
 	
Authorized Access only
   This system is the property of So-&-So-
Enterprise.
   UNAUTHORIZED ACCESS TO THIS DEVICE IS
PROHIBITED.
   You must have explicit permission to access
this
   device. All activities performed on this
device
   are logged. Any violations of access policy
will result
   in disciplinary action.
 	
Enter the security banner {Put the banner
between
k and k, where k is any character}:
#This system is the property of Rothson
Educational Consulting.
UNAUTHORIZED ACCESS TO THIS DEVICE IS
PROHIBITED!#
	Allows you to create a security banner
	
	NOTE: Creating a security banner here is the same as using the **banner** command in global configuration mode

Enable secret is either not configured or is the same as enable password Enter the new enable secret: **xxxxxxxx** Confirm the enable secret : **xxxxxxxx**	AutoSecure checks to see if the enable secret password is set, or is the same as the enable password. If either is true, you are prompted to enter a new enable secret password.

`Enter the new enable password:` **xxxx**
`% Password too short - must be at least 6`
`characters. Password configuration failed`
`Enter the new enable password:` **xxxxxxx**
`Confirm the enable password:` **xxxxxxx**
	Prompts you to enter a new enable password, which must be at least six characters

`Configuring AAA local authentication`
`Configuring Console, Aux and VTY lines for`
`local authentication, exec-timeout, and`
`transport`
`Securing device against Login Attacks`
`Configure the following parameters`
	Checks for AAA local authentication and whether a local user account exists. If neither is true, you are prompted to enter a username and password.

`Blocking Period when Login Attack detected:` **300**	Sets the blocking period, in seconds—known as the *quiet period*
`Maximum Login failures with the device:` **3**	Sets the maximum number of failed login attempts that triggers the quiet period
`Maximum time period for crossing the failed` `login attempts:` **60**	Sets the duration of time in which the allowed number of failed login attempts must be made before the blocking period is triggered
`Configure SSH server? [yes]:` **y**	Configures SSH functionality If you answer *yes*, AutoSecure automatically configures the SSH timeout to 60 seconds and the number of SSH authentication retries to two. If there is no hostname or domain name in the current configuration, you will be prompted to enter one here.

`Configuring interface specific AutoSecure`
`services`
`Disabling the following ip services on all`
`interfaces:`
 	
  `no ip redirects`
  `no ip proxy-arp`
  `no ip unreachables`
  `no ip directed-broadcast`
  `no ip mask-reply`
`Disabling mop on Ethernet interfaces`
	AutoSecure will automatically disable these services on all router interfaces.

`Securing Forwarding plane services…`
 	
`Enabling CEF (This might impact the memory`
`requirements for your platform)`
 	
`Enabling unicast rpf on all interfaces`
`connected to internet`
	AutoSecure will secure the forwarding plane.
	Enables CEF (or dCEF if supported))
	
	Enables unicast RPF (if supported)
	You are asked to enable the CBAC Firewall feature here if it is supported on the router.

`This is the configuration generated:`
 	
`no service finger`
`no service pad`
`no service udp-small-servers`
`no service tcp-small-servers`
`service password-encryption`
`service tcp-keepalives-in`
`service tcp-keepalives-out`
`.`
`.`
`.`
`.`
`end`
	A summary is then listed for you to review.

Apply this configuration to running-config? [yes]: **y** Applying the config generated to running-config The name for the keys will be: 2821.yourdomain.com % The key modulus size is 1024 bits % Generating 1024 bit RSA keys, keys will be non-exportable…[OK] 2821#	Type **y** or press **Enter** to accept the configuration and apply it to the running configuration.

Optional AutoSecure Parameters

2821Router#**auto secure management**	Secures only the management plane
2821Router#**auto secure forwarding**	Secures only the forwarding plane
2821Router#**auto secure no-interact**	Specifies that the user will not be prompted for any interactive configurations **NOTE:** Any parameters that need interactive dialog will not be configured, such as usernames or passwords.
2821Router#**auto secure full**	Specifies to prompt the user for all interactive questions **NOTE:** This is the same as the **auto secure** command shown in the previous example.
2821Router#**auto secure ntp**	Specifies the configuration of the NTP feature

`2821Router#`**`auto secure login`**	Specifies the configuration of the Login feature
`2821Router#`**`auto secure ssh`**	Specifies the configuration of the SSH feature
`2821Router#`**`auto secure firewall`**	Specifies the configuration of the Firewall feature
`2821Router#`**`auto secure tcp-intercept`**	Specifies the configuration of the TCP-intercept feature

WARNING: If AutoSecure fails to complete its operation, you may end up with a corrupt running configuration. Depending on your release of IOS, the steps for recovery are as follows:

In Cisco IOS Release 12.3(8)T and later—Pre-AutoSecure configuration is stored in flash under the filename **pre_autosec.cfg**. Use the command **configure replace flash:pre_cautosec.cfg** to roll back the router to the pre-AutoSecure configuration. This will apply all necessary additions and deletions to replace the current running configuration (which may be corrupt) with the contents of the specified configuration file, which is assumed to be a complete configuration, not a partial configuration.

In Cisco IOS releases prior to 12.3(8T)—Save the running configuration to NVRAM first with the **copy running-config startup-config** command before running AutoSecure. There is no rollback feature available.

Locking Down Routers with Cisco SDM

There are two options for securing your router using Cisco Router and Security Device Manager (SDM):

- **SDM Security Audit Wizard**—Compares router configurations to a predefined checklist of best practices. After comparison, a Report Card is displayed that shows a list of possible security problems. You then choose the vulnerabilities that you would like to lock down.
- **One-Step Lockdown**—Initiates an automatic lockdown using recommended settings.

SDM Security Audit Wizard

As shown in Figure 5-1, from the home page of SDM, click the **Configure** button at the top of the page, and then click the **Security Audit** icon in the Tasks toolbar.

Figure 5-1 Main Security Audit Window

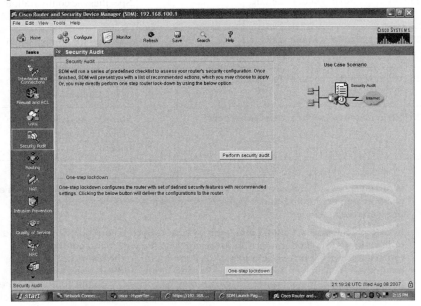

From this page you have two options: Perform Security Audit and One-Step Lockdown. Click **Perform Security Audit** to start the Security Audit Wizard, shown in Figure 5-2.

Figure 5-2 Security Audit Wizard

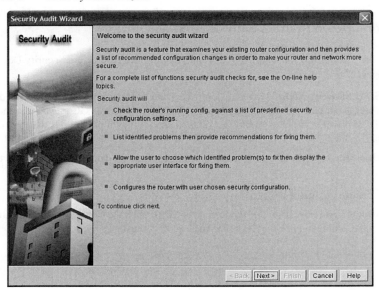

To continue with the wizard, click **Next**. This takes you to the second page of the wizard, the Interface Configuration page, shown in Figure 5-3. Choose your inside (trusted) and outside (untrusted) interfaces, and click **Next** to continue.

Figure 5-3   Security Audit Interface Configuration

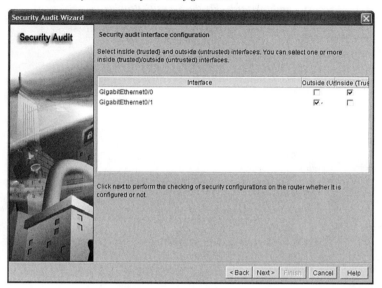

From here the Security Audit Wizard tests your router configuration and prepares a report of its findings, shown in Figure 5-4.

Figure 5-4   Security Audit Report

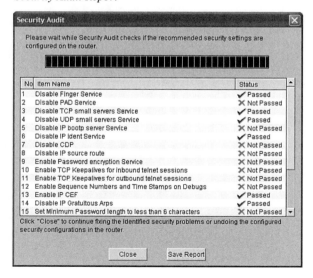

You have two choices at this point. Click **Close** to go on and fix the identified security problems, or click **Save Report** to save a copy of the report. Clicking Close opens the page shown in Figure 5-5, where you are given the option to either fix problems or undo something currently configured.

Figure 5-5   Security Audit Wizard—Fix the Security Problems

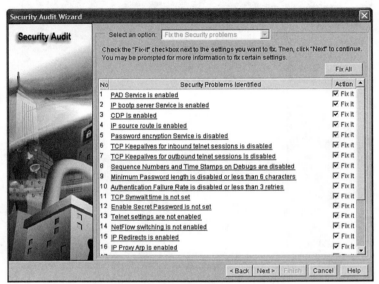

Depending on what you have chosen on the previous page, you are given wizard pages that allow you to correct these security violations. Figure 5-6 shows the page for entering the enable secret password.

Figure 5-6   Security Audit Wizard—Enable Secret Password

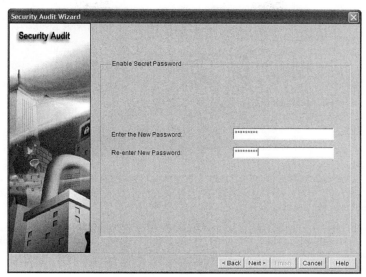

Figure 5-7 shows the Summary page of the Security Audit Wizard, which displays the changes that will be delivered to the router. After reviewing and verifying the list, click **Finish** to send these changes to the router. Figure 5-8 shows the delivery status after the commands have been sent to the router.

Figure 5-7   Security Audit Wizard—Summary

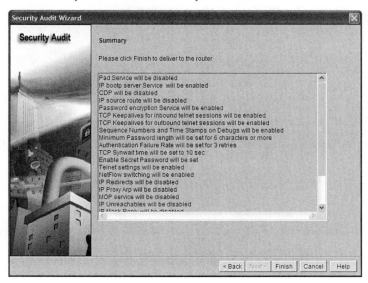

Figure 5-8   *Commands Delivery Status*

One-Step Lockdown

Cisco SDM also provides an easy One-Step Lockdown procedure for many security features. This option tests the router for potential problems and then automatically makes any necessary changes. Figure 5-9 shows the SDM Warning that appears if you click the **One-Step Lockdown** button on the main Security Audit page.

Figure 5-9   *One-Step Lockdown—SDM Warning*

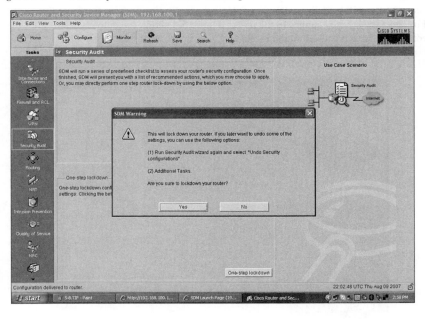

Click the **Yes** button on the SDM Warning to get a summary of what the One-Step Lockdown will do to the router, shown in Figure 5-10. Click the **Deliver** button to move to the Commands Delivery Status dialog box, shown in Figure 5-11.

Figure 5-10   One-Step Lockdown

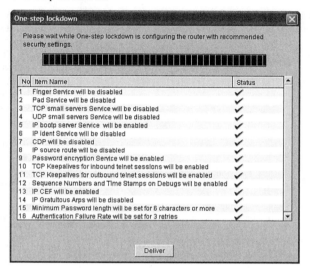

Figure 5-11   Commands Delivery Status

Setting Cisco Passwords and Password Security

`Router(config)#`**`enable password cisco`**	Sets the enable password to cisco
`Router(config)#`**`enable secret class`**	Sets the enable secret password to **class** **CAUTION:** The enable secret password is encrypted by default. The enable password is not. For this reason, recommended practice is that you never use the enable password. Use the enable secret password only in a router configuration. **CAUTION:** You should not set both the enable password and the enable secret password to the same password. Although Cisco IOS will warn you to change your enable secret password, it will accept the same password. Doing do defeats the use of the encryption feature of the enable secret password.
`Router(config)#`**`line console 0`**	Enters console line configuration mode
`Router(config-line)#`**`password darktower`**	Sets the console mode password to **darktower**
`Router(config-line)#`**`login`**	Enables password checking at login
`Router(config)#`**`line vty 0 4`**	Enters line vty mode for all five vty lines
`Router(config-line)#`**`password iscwguide`**	Sets vty password to **iscwguide**

`Router(config-line)#`**`login`**	Enables password checking at login
`Router(config)#`**`line aux 0`**	Enters auxiliary line mode
`Router(config-line)#`**`password backdoor`**	Sets console mode password to **backdoor**
`Router(config-line)#`**`login`**	Enables password checking at login
`Router(config)#`**`service password-encryption`**	Applies a weak encryption to passwords **NOTE:** The **service password-encryption** command uses a Cisco proprietary algorithm based on the Vigenere cipher (as indicated by the number 7 when viewing the configuration). This is considered to be a relatively weak algorithm, and can be cracked easily. Therefore it is imperative to use other methods to secure your routers than just password encryption.

`Router(config)#no service password-encryption`	Turns off password encryption **NOTE:** If you use the **service password-encryption** command to encrypt your passwords, and then turn password encryption off with the **no service password-encryption** command, your passwords will remain encrypted; new passwords will be unencrypted, except for the enable secret password, which is always encrypted with the MD5 algorithm.
`Router(config)#security passwords min-length 10`	Sets a requirement for all user/enable passwords to be a minimum of ten characters in length **NOTE:** This command was introduced in Cisco IOS Release 12.3(1). Range is from 0 to 16 characters. Existing router passwords are not affected by this command. It is highly recommended to set a minimum password length of at least ten characters.
`Router(config)#username roland password darktower`	Creates a locally stored password of darktower for the username roland. The password is unencrypted but can be encrypted with the **service password-encryption** command.

`Router(config)#`**`username roland password 7`** **`darktower`**	Creates a locally stored password of darktower for the username roland. The password is encrypted with the weak Vigenere algorithm.
`Router(config)#`**`username roland secret 0`** **`darktower`**	Enables enhanced username password security that uses MD5 hashing on the plaintext password **darktower**
`Router(config)#`**`username roland secret 5`** **`$1$ExxV$YMPap5SrXimAKcWilh2Sp1`**	Enables enhanced username password security that uses a previously encrypted MD5 secret **NOTE:** MD5 encryption is considered to be a strong encryption method and is therefore not retrievable. You cannot use MD5 encryption with protocols that require plaintext passwords, such as CHAP.

Securing ROMMON

`Router(config)#`**`no service password-recovery`**	Disables password-recovery capability at the system console **NOTE:** This feature is not available on all platforms. Use Cisco Feature Navigator on Cisco.com to ensure that it is available on your platform.

CAUTION: Using the **no service password-recovery** command prevents all access to ROMMON. You cannot perform a password recovery with the Break sequence to enter ROMMON.

A valid Cisco IOS image should be in flash memory before this command is entered. If you do not have a valid image in flash, you will not be able to use the ROMMON> **xmodem** command to load a new flash image.

NOTE: To recover a device once the **no service password-recovery** command has been entered, press the Break key within 5 seconds after the image decompresses during the boot. You are prompted to confirm the Break key action. When you confirm the action, the startup configuration is erased, the password-recovery procedure is enabled, and the router boots with the factory default configuration.

If you do not confirm the Break key action, the router boots normally with the No Service Password-Recovery feature enabled.

Setting a Login Failure Rate

`Router(config)#`**`security authentication failure`** **`rate 5 log`**	Configures the number of unsuccessful login attempts allowed to five **NOTE:** This command is available starting with Cisco IOS Release 12.3(1). The default is ten attempts before initiating a 15-second delay. The range is from 2–1024. The **log** keyword is required because a syslog event will be generated under the name TOOMANY_AUTHFAILS.

`Router(config)#`**`login block-for 120 attempts 3 within 100`**	Blocks access for 120 seconds after three failed login attempts within a 100-second period **NOTE:** This command was introduced in Cisco IOS Release 12.3(4)T. The duration of time in which login attempts are denied is known as the *quiet period*. The quiet period can be set from 1–65535 seconds. Failed login attempts range from 1–65535 tries. The amount of time in which the failed login attempts must be made before the quiet period is triggered ranges from 1–65535 seconds. **NOTE:** You must issue the **login block-for** command before using any other **login** commands. **NOTE:** All login attempts made via Telnet, Secure Shell (SSH), and HTTP are denied during the quiet period; no ACLs are exempt from the login period until the **login quiet-mode access-class** command is issued.
`Router(config)#`**`login delay 10`**	Sets a delay between successive login attempts **NOTE:** If the **login delay** command is not used, a default time of 1 second is set after the **login block-for** command is configured.

| `Router#show login` | Displays login parameters |
| `Router#show login failures` | Displays login failures |

Setting Timeouts

| `Router(config)#line console 0` | Moves to console line configuration mode |
| `Router(config-line)#exec-timeout 2 30` | Sets the console to log out after 2 minutes and 30 seconds of inactivity

NOTE: The **exec-timeout** command is read as minutes and seconds. **exec-timeout 5 30** means 5 minutes and 30 seconds. **exec-timeout 0 20** means 20 seconds. The default is 10 minutes. **exec-timeout 0 1** is read as 1 second, and thus 1 second of inactivity triggers a logout. |

Setting Multiple Privilege Levels

| `Router(config)#privilege exec level 2 ping` | Assigns the **ping** command to privilege level 2 |
| `Router(config)#privilege exec level 7 clear counters` | Assigns the **clear counters** command to privilege level 7 |

`Router(config)#`**`privilege exec all level 7`** **`reload`**	Changes the privilege level of the **reload** command from level 15 to level 7 **NOTE:** There are 16 levels of privileges that can be used on Cisco routers. Level 0 is predefined for user-level access privileges. Level 15 is predefined for enable mode—a user at level 15 can configure and monitor every part of the router. Levels 1–14 are customizable.

Configuring Banner Messages

`Router(config)#`**`banner motd %`** **`WARNING:  This system is the property of`** **`Rothson Educational Consulting.  UNAUTHORIZED`** **`ACCESS TO THIS DEVICE IS PROHIBITED!`** **`%`**	Creates a message-of-the-day (MOTD) banner **NOTE:** In this example and the following example, % is a *delimiting character*. The delimiting character must surround the banner message and can be any character if it is not a character used within the body of the message.

	NOTE: The MOTD banner is displayed on all terminals and is useful for sending messages that affect all users. Use the **no banner motd** command to disable the MOTD banner. The MOTD banner will be displayed before the login prompt and the login banner, if one has been created.

`Router(config)#`**`banner login %`**
`Authorized Personnel Only! Please enter your`
`username and password.`
`%`
	Creates a login banner
	
	NOTE: The login banner is displayed before the username and password login prompts. Use the **no banner login** command to disable the login banner. The MOTD banner will be displayed before the login banner.

TIP: Four valid wildcards can be used within the message section of the **banner** command:

- **$(hostname)**—Displays the hostname for the router
- **$(domain)**—Displays the domain name for the router
- **$(line)**—Displays the vty or tty (asynchronous) line number
- **$(line-desc)**—Displays the description attached to the line

```
Router(config)#banner motd %
```
```
You are connected to $(hostname) of the Rothson Educational
Consulting network.  Authorized Personnel Only!
%
```

Role-Based CLI

The traditional approach of limiting CLI access based on privilege levels and enable passwords is considered to be very weak in terms of providing control. For example, there was no access control to specific interfaces, and commands placed on higher privilege levels could not be reused for lower privileged users. Role-Based CLI allows for the creation of a *view*, which is a set of commands and configuration capabilities that provides select or partial access to IOS commands.

2821(config)#**aaa new-model**	Enables AAA, which must be configured to create a view
2821(config)#**exit**	Returns to privileged mode
2821#**disable**	Returns to user mode
2821>**enable view** Password:**xxxxxx** %PARSER-6-VIEW_SWITCH: successfully set to view 'root' 2821#	Enters root view, which allows users to configure CLI views Prompts you to enter the enable secret password
2821#**configure terminal**	Moves to global configuration mode
2821(config)#**parser view first** %PARSER-6-VIEW_CREATED: view 'first' successfully created.	Creates a view named first and enters view configuration mode
2821(config-view)#**secret firstpassword**	Associates the CLI view with a secret password

`2821(config-view)#secret 5` `$1$ExxV$YMPap5SrXimAKcWilh2Sp1`	Associates the CLI view with a secret password— **5** indicates the password is encrypted with MD5— works for me **NOTE:** You must associate a password with a view. If you do not associate a password, and you attempt to add commands to the view via the **commands** command, a system message such as the following will be displayed: `%Password not set for view <viewname>.`
`2821(config-view)#commands exec include show version`	Adds the EXEC-level command **show version** to this view
`2821(config-view)#commands exec include configure terminal`	Adds the EXEC-level command **configure terminal** to this view
`2821(config-view)#commands exec include all show ip`	Adds all of the EXEC-level commands that start with **show ip** to this view
`2821(config-view)#commands exec include-exclusive show controllers`	Adds the EXEC-level command **show controller** to this view only. This command cannot be added to other views.
`2821(config-view)#commands exec exclude show protocols`	Excludes the EXEC-level command **show protocols** from this view. This command cannot be accessed when logged in under this view.

`2821(config-view)#exit`	Exits view configuration mode
`2821(config)#exit`	Exits global configuration mode
`2821#`	
`2821#enable view first`	Prompts the user for a password in order to allow the user to access the view named first
`2821#show parser view`	Displays information about the view that the user is currently in

`2821#?`
`Exec commands:`
`  configure    Enter configuration mode`
`  enable       Turn on privileged commands`
`  exit         Exit from the EXEC`
`  show         Show running system`
`               information`
	Issuing a question mark (**?**) command here shows you what commands are available to use in this view

Secure Configuration Files

The Cisco IOS Resilient Configuration feature enables a router to secure and maintain a working copy of the running image and configuration so that those files can withstand malicious attempts to erase the contents of persistent storage in NVRAM and flash.

The Cisco IOS Resilient Configuration feature is available only on platforms that support a Personal Computer Memory Card International Association (PCMCIA) Advanced Technology Attachment (ATA) disk. There must be enough space on the storage device to accommodate at least one Cisco IOS image and a copy of the running configuration.

Secured files will not appear on the output of a **dir** command issued from an executive shell because the Cisco IOS File System (IFS) prevents secure files in a directory from being listed. ROM Monitor (ROMMON) mode does not have any such restriction and can be used to list and boot secured files. The running image and running configuration archives will not be visible in the Cisco IOS **dir** command output.

`Router(config)#`**`secure boot-image`**	Enables IOS image resilience and secures the running image
`Router(config)#`**`secure boot-config`**	Stores a secure copy of the primary bootset in persistent storage
`Router(config)#`**`exit`**	Returns to privileged EXEC mode
`Router#`**`show secure bootset`**	Displays the status of configuration resilience and the primary bootset filename

Tips for Using Access Control Lists

The Cisco Access Control List (ACL) is one of the most commonly used features in the IOS. ACLs can be used not only for packet filtering but also for selecting specific types of traffic for analysis. The following is a list of tips to consider when using ACLs:

- If you want to deny or permit the entire IP protocol stack, use a standard ACL. If you want to deny or permit only part of the stack—only open up a single port, for example—use an extended ACL.

- Standard ACLs use numbers 1 to 99 and 1300 to 1999. Extended ACLs use numbers 100 to 100 and 2000 to 2699. If you are using names for your ACLs, the names cannot contain spaces or punctuation, and must begin with an alphabetic character.

- ACLs applied in an *inbound* direction apply to packets that are received on the router interface and are trying to travel *into* or *through* the router to a different exit interface. ACLs applied in an *outbound* direction apply to packets that are trying to leave the router through an exit interface.

- Disable unused services, ports, or protocols. If no one needs them, turn them off. If someone needs access to them, use an ACL.

- You can have only one ACL per interface, per direction, per protocol. Therefore, combine your requirements into a single ACL.

- All Cisco ACLs end with the *implicit deny* statement that denies everything. You will not see this statement in your ACL, but it does exist.

- Put your more-specific ACL statements at the top of your ACLs—if you have an ACL statement blocking all UDP traffic, and then a second statement that permits SNMP, the second statement will never be acted upon.

- Unless you use sequence numbers in your ACL, new ACL statements will be appended to the end of the ACL. Depending on the existing ACL statements, these new lines may never be acted upon. If necessary, write your ACLs in Notepad or some other text editor, verify them on paper first for proper syntax and order, and then cut-and-paste them into your router configuration.

- Router-generated packets are not subject to outbound ACL statements on the source router. Use the **extended ping** utility and test your ACLs by using a different source address.

- Place an extended ACL as close as possible to the source of traffic that the ACL is filtering. This is to prevent packets you know are going to be filtered out from traveling across your network, utilizing bandwidth.

- Place standard ACLs as close as possible to the destination. Placing them closer to the source may prevent legitimate packets from reaching their destinations.

Using ACLs to Filter Network Traffic to Mitigate Threats

Figure 5-12 shows the network topology for the configurations that follow, which demonstrate how to use ACLs to filter network traffic to mitigate threats to your network.

Figure 5-12   Network Edge

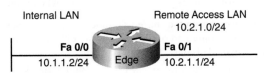

IP Address Spoofing: Inbound

As a rule, do not allow any IP packets that contain the source address of any internal hosts or networks inbound to a private network.

`Edge(config)#access-list 101 deny ip 10.2.1.0` `0.0.0.255 any log`	Denies any packet with a source IP address of 10.2.1.x from reaching any destination, and logs any instance in which this statement was used
`Edge(config)#access-list 101 deny ip 127.0.0.0` `0.255.255.255 any log`	Denies any packet with a source IP address of 127.x.x.x from reaching any destination, and logs any instance in which this statement was used

`Edge(config)#`**`access-list 101 deny ip 0.0.0.0`** **`0.255.255.255 any log`**	Denies any packet with a source IP address of 0.x.x.x from reaching any destination, and logs any instance in which this statement was used
`Edge(config)#`**`access-list 101 deny ip`** **`172.16.0.0 0.15.255.255 any log`**	Denies any packet with a source IP address of 172.16.0.0–172.31.255.255 from reaching any destination, and logs any instance in which this statement was used
`Edge(config)#`**`access-list 101 deny ip`** **`192.168.0.0 0.0.255.255 any log`**	Denies any packet with a source IP address of 192.168.x.x from reaching any destination, and logs any instance in which this statement was used
`Edge(config)#`**`access-list 101 deny ip 224.0.0.0`** **`31.255.255.255 any log`**	Denies any packet with a source IP address of 224–239.x.x.x from reaching any destination, and logs any instance in which this statement was used
`Edge(config)#`**`access-list 101 deny ip host`** **`255.255.255.255 any log`**	Denies any packet with a source IP address of 255.255.255.255 from reaching any destination, and logs any instance in which this statement was used
`Edge(config)#`**`access-list 101 permit ip any`** **`10.2.1.0 0.0.0.255`**	Permits any address to travel to the 10.2.1.0/24 network
`Edge(config)#`**`interface fastethernet 0/0`**	Moves to interface configuration mode

`Edge(config-if)#ip access-group 101 in`	Takes all access list lines that are defined as being part of group 101 and applies them in an inbound manner
`Edge(config-if)#exit`	Returns to global configuration mode
`Edge(config)#`	

IP Address Spoofing: Outbound

As a rule, you should not allow any outbound IP packets with a source address other than a valid IP address of the internal network. Refer to Figure 5-12 for the network topology upon which the following configurations are based.

`Edge(config)#access-list 102 permit ip 10.2.1.0 0.0.0.255 any`	Permits packets with a source address of 10.2.1.x to travel to the internal network
`Edge(config)#access-list 102 deny ip any any log`	Denies all packets from any source to reach any destination, and logs any instance in which this statement was used **NOTE:** The second line of this access list is almost identical to the implicit deny statement. So why use it? The statement also has the **log** argument added to it, which the implicit deny statement does not have. Although the implicit deny statement could have been used here, there would be no record of how many times a packet was filtered out by the implicit deny statement.

`Edge(config)#`**`interface fastethernet 0/1`**	Moves to interface configuration mode
`Edge(config-if)#`**`ip access-group 102 out`**	Takes all access list lines that are defined as being part of group 102 and applies them in an outbound manner
`Edge(config-if)#`**`exit`**	Returns to global configuration mode
`Edge(config)#`	

DoS TCP SYN Attacks: Blocking External Attacks

TCP SYN attacks involve sending large numbers of TCP SYN packets, often from a spoofed source, into the internal network, which results in the flooding of the TCP connection queues of the receiving nodes. Refer to Figure 5-12 for the network topology upon which the following configurations are based.

The following ACL prevents inbound packets, with the SYN flag set, from entering the router. However, the ACL does allow TCP responses from the outside network for TCP connections that originated on the inside network (keyword **established**). The **established** option is used for the TCP protocol only. This option indicates return traffic from an established connection. A match occurs if the TCP datagram has the ACK control bit set.

`Edge(config)#`**`access-list 103 permit tcp any`** **`10.2.1.0 0.0.0.255 established`**	Permits packets with the ACK control bit set to enter the router
`Edge(config)#`**`access-list 103 deny ip any any`** **`log`**	Denies all other packets from entering the router, and logs any instance in which this statement was used
`Edge(config)#`**`interface fastethernet 0/0`**	Moves to interface configuration mode
`Edge(config-if)#`**`ip access-group 103 in`**	Takes all access list lines that are defined as being part of group 103 and applies them in an inbound manner

`Edge(config-if)#exit`	Returns to global configuration mode
`Edge(config)#`	

DoS TCP SYN Attacks: Using TCP Intercept

TCP Intercept is a very effective tool for protecting internal network hosts from external TCP SYN attacks. TCP Intercept protects internal hosts from SYN flood attacks by intercepting and validating TCP connection requests before the requests reach the hosts. Valid connections (those connections established within the configured thresholds) are passed on to the host. Invalid connection attempts are dropped.

> **CAUTION:** Because TCP Intercept examines every TCP connection attempt, TCP Intercept can impose a performance burden on your routers. Always test for any performance problems before using TCP Intercept in a production environment.

Refer to Figure 5-12 for the network topology upon which the following configurations are based.

`Edge(config)#ip tcp intercept list 104`	Enables TCP intercept. Router IOS will intercept packets for all TCP servers based on information provided by ACL 104.
`Edge(config)#access-list 104 permit tcp any 10.2.1.0 0.0.0.255`	Permits packets with any source address to travel to the 10.2.1.0 network
`Edge(config)#access-list 104 deny ip any any log`	Denies all other packets from entering the router, and logs any instance in which this statement was used
`Edge(config)#interface fastethernet 0/0`	Moves to interface configuration mode
`Edge(config-if)#ip access-group 104 in`	Takes all access list lines that are defined as being part of group 104 and applies them in an inbound manner

`Edge(config-if)#`**`exit`**	Returns to global configuration mode
`Edge(config)#`	

DoS Smurf Attacks

Smurf attacks consist of large numbers of ICMP packets sent to a router subnet broadcast address using a spoofed source IP address from that same subnet. Some routers may be configured to forward these broadcasts to other routers in the protected network, and this process causes performance degradation.

> **NOTE:** Cisco IOS Release 12.0 and later now has the **no ip directed-broadcast** feature enabled by default, which prevents this type of ICMP attack.

Refer to Figure 5-12 for the network topology upon which the following configurations are based.

`Edge(config)#`**`access-list 105 deny ip any host 10.2.1.255 log`**	Denies any packet with a destination address of 10.2.1.255
`Edge(config)#`**`access-list 105 permit ip any 10.2.1.0 0.0.0.255 log`**	Permits packets to any other destination address on the 10.2.1.0 network, and logs any instance in which this statement was used
`Edge(config)#`**`access-list 106 deny ip any host 10.1.1.255 log`**	Denies any a packet with a destination address of 10.1.1.255
`Edge(config)#`**`access-list 106 permit ip any 10.1.1.0 0.0.0.255 log`**	Permits packets to any other destination address on the 10.1.1.0 network, and logs any instance in which this statement was used
`Edge(config)#`**`interface fastethernet 0/0`**	Moves to interface configuration mode

`Edge(config-if)#ip access-group 105 in`	Takes all access list lines that are defined as being part of group 105 and applies them in an inbound manner
`Edge(config-if)#exit`	Returns to global configuration mode
`Edge(config)#interface fastethernet 0/1`	Moves to interface configuration mode
`Edge(config-if)#ip access-group 106 in`	Takes all access list lines that are defined as being part of group 106 and applies them in an inbound manner
`Edge(config-if)#exit`	Returns to global configuration mode
`Edge(config)#`	

Filtering ICMP Messages: Inbound

There are several Internet Control Message Protocol (ICMP) message types that attackers can use against your network. Programs use some of these messages; others are used for network management and so are automatically generated by the router.

ICMP echo packets can be used to discover subnets and hosts on the protected network and can also be used to generate DoS floods. ICMP redirect messages can be used to alter host routing tables. The router should block both ICMP echo and redirect messages that are inbound.

Refer to Figure 5-12 for the network topology upon which the following configurations are based.

`Edge(config)#access-list 107 deny icmp any any echo log`	Blocks echo packets from anywhere going to anywhere, and logs any instance in which this statement was used
`Edge(config)#access-list 107 deny icmp any any redirect log`	Blocks redirect packets from anywhere going to anywhere, and logs any instance in which this statement was used

`Edge(config)#`**`access-list 107 deny icmp any any`** **`mask-request log`**	Blocks mask-request packets from anywhere going to anywhere, and logs any instance in which this statement was used
`Edge(config)#`**`access-list 107 permit icmp any`** **`10.2.1.0 0.0.0.255`**	Permits all other ICMP messages from traveling to the 10.2.1.0 network
`Edge(config)#`**`interface fastethernet 0/0`**	Moves to interface configuration mode
`Edge(config-if)#`**`ip access-group 107 in`**	Takes all access list lines that are defined as being part of group 107 and applies them in an inbound manner
`Edge(config-if)#`**`exit`**	Returns to global configuration mode
`Edge(config)#`	

Filtering ICMP Messages: Outbound

The following ICMP messages are required for proper network operation and should be allowed outbound:

- **Echo**—Allows users to ping external hosts
- **Parameter problem**—Informs host of packet header problems
- **Packet too big**—Required for packet maximum transmission unit (MTU) discovery
- **Source quench**—Throttles down traffic when necessary

As a general rule, you should block all other ICMP message types that are outbound.

Refer to Figure 5-12 for the network topology upon which the following configurations are based.

`Edge(config)#`**`access-list 108 permit icmp`** **`10.2.1.0 0.0.0.255 any echo`**	Permits echo packets from 10.2.1.x going to anywhere
`Edge(config)#`**`access-list 108 permit icmp`** **`10.2.1.0 0.0.0.255 any parameter-problem`**	Permits parameter problem packets from 10.2.1.x going to anywhere

`Edge(config)#access-list 108 permit icmp` `10.2.1.0 0.0.0.255 any packet-too-big`	Permits packet-too-big packets from 10.2.1.x going to anywhere
`Edge(config)#access-list 108 permit icmp` `10.2.1.0 0.0.0.255 any source-quench`	Permits source-quench packets from 10.2.1.x going to anywhere
`Edge(config)#access-list 108 deny icmp any any` `log`	Denies all other ICMP packets from anywhere going to anywhere, and logs any instance in which this statement was used
`Edge(config)#interface fastethernet 0/1`	Moves to interface configuration mode
`Edge(config-if)#ip access-group 108 in`	Takes all access list lines that are defined as being part of group 108 and applies them in an inbound manner
`Edge(config-if)#exit`	Returns to global configuration mode
`Edge(config)#`	

Filtering UDP Traceroute Messages

Traceroute displays the IP addresses of the routers that a packet encounters along the packet path (hops) from source to destination. Attackers can use ICMP responses to the UDP traceroute packets to discover subnets and hosts on the protected network.

As a rule, you should block all inbound traceroute UDP messages (UDP ports 33400 to 34400).

Refer to Figure 5-12 for the network topology upon which the following configurations are based.

`Edge(config)#`**`access-list 109 deny udp any any`** **`range 33400 34400 log`**	Denies all packets with ports in the range of 33400–34400, and logs any instance in which this statement was used **NOTE:** Make sure that the range of ports that you specify in this statement does not filter out any packets that you want to travel through the network.
`Edge(config)#`**`access-list 109 permit ip any`** **`10.1.1.0 0.0.0.255 log`**	Permits any IP packets from anywhere destined for 10.1.1.x, and logs any instance in which this statement was used
`Edge(config)#`**`interface fastethernet 0/1`**	Moves to interface configuration mode
`Edge(config-if)#`**`ip access-group 109 in`**	Takes all access list lines that are defined as being part of group 109 and applies them in an inbound manner
`Edge(config-if)#`**`exit`**	Returns to global configuration mode
`Edge(config)#`	

Mitigating Dedicated DoS Attacks with ACLs

Generally, routers cannot prevent all DDoS attacks, but they can help reduce the number of occurrences of attacks by building ACLs that filter known attack ports. Methods that you use to block DDoS by blocking selected ports aim at stopping TRIN00, Stacheldraht, Trinity v3, and SubSeven. ACL rules are generally applied to inbound and outbound traffic between the protected network and the Internet.

RFC 2827 recommends that ISPs police their customer traffic by dropping traffic that enters their networks from a source address that the customer network is not legitimately using. The filtering includes, but is not limited to, traffic whose source address is a "Martian address"—a reserved address that includes any address within 0.0.0.0/8, 10.0.0.0/8, 127.0.0.0/8, 169.254.0.0/16, 172.16.0.0/12, 192.168.0.0/16, 224.0.0.0/4, or 240.0.0.0/4.

RFC 3704 is the update to RFC 2827.

Mitigating TRIN00

TRIN00 is a SYN DDoS attack. The attack method is a UDP flood.

The TRIN00 attack sets up communications between clients, handlers, and agents using these ports:

- 1524 TCP
- 27665 TCP
- 27444 UCP
- 31335 UCP

The mitigation tactic for the TRIN00 attack is to block both interfaces in the *inbound* direction. The goal is to prevent infected outside systems from sending messages to an internal network and to prevent any infected internal systems from sending messages out of an internal network to the vulnerable ports.

Refer to Figure 5-12 for the network topology upon which the following configurations are based.

`Edge(config)#access-list 150 deny tcp any any eq 1524 log`	Denies any TCP traffic from any network from going to any network through port 1524, and logs any instance in which this statement was used
`Edge(config)#access-list 150 deny tcp any any eq 27444 log`	Denies any TCP traffic from any network from going to any network through port 27444, and logs any instance in which this statement was used
`Edge(config)#access-list 150 deny tcp any any eq 27665 log`	Denies any TCP traffic from any network from going to any network through port 27665, and logs any instance in which this statement was used

`Edge(config)#`**`access-list 150 deny tcp any any`** **`eq 31335 log`**	Denies any TCP traffic from any network from going to any network through port 31335, and logs any instance in which this statement was used
`Edge(config)#`**`access-list 150 permit ip any any`**	Allows all other traffic through
`Edge(config)#`**`interface fastethernet 0/0`**	Moves to interface configuration mode
`Edge(config-if)#`**`ip access-group 150 in`**	Takes all access list lines that are defined as being part of group 150 and applies them in an inbound manner
`Edge(config-if)#`**`exit`**	Returns to global configuration mode
`Edge(config)#`**`interface fastethernet 0/1`**	Moves to interface configuration mode
`Edge(config-if)#`**`ip access-group 150 in`**	Takes all access list lines that are defined as being part of group 150 and applies them in an inbound manner
`Edge(config-if)#`**`exit`**	Returns to global configuration mode
`Edge(config)#`	

Mitigating Stacheldraht

Stacheldraht is a DDoS tool that appeared in 1999 and combines features of TRIN00 and Tribe Flood Network (TFN). Possible Stacheldraht attacks are similar to the attacks of TFN; namely, ICMP flood, SYN flood, UDP flood, and smurf attacks.

A Stacheldraht attack sets up communication between clients, handlers, and agents using these ports:

- 16660 TCP
- 65000 TCP

Refer to Figure 5-12 for the network topology upon which the following configurations are based.

`Edge(config)#access-list 151 deny tcp any any eq 16660 log`	Denies any TCP traffic from any network from going to any network through port 16660, and logs any instance in which this statement was used
`Edge(config)#access-list 151 deny tcp any any eq 65000 log`	Denies any TCP traffic from any network from going to any network through port 65000, and logs any instance in which this statement was used **NOTE:** The ports listed above are the default ports for the Stacheldraht tool. Use these ports for orientation and example only, because the port numbers can easily be changed.
`Edge(config)#access-list 151 permit ip any any`	Allows all other traffic through
`Edge(config)#interface fastethernet 0/0`	Moves to interface configuration mode
`Edge(config-if)#ip access-group 151 in`	Takes all access list lines that are defined as being part of group 151 and applies them in an inbound manner
`Edge(config-if)#exit`	Returns to global configuration mode
`Edge(config)#interface fastethernet 0/1`	Moves to interface configuration mode

`Edge(config-if)#`**`ip access-group 151 in`**	Takes all access list lines that are defined as being part of group 151 and applies them in an inbound manner
`Edge(config-if)#`**`exit`**	Returns to global configuration mode
`Edge(config)#`	

NOTE: If your port numbers change, and they can change, defending against this attack is rather challenging and means constant monitoring of the network.

Mitigating Trinity v3

Trinity is capable of launching several types of flooding attacks on a victim site, including UDP, fragment, SYN, restore (RST), acknowledgement (ACK), and other floods. Communication from the handler or intruder to the agent is accomplished via Internet Relay Chat (IRC) or ICQ from AOL. Trinity appears to use primarily TCP port 6667 and also has a backdoor program that listens on TCP port 33270.

Refer to Figure 5-12 for the network topology upon which the following configurations are based.

`Edge(config)#`**`access-list 152 deny tcp any any eq 6667 log`**	Denies any TCP traffic from any network from going to any network through port 6667, and logs any instance in which this statement was used
`Edge(config)#`**`access-list 152 deny tcp any any eq 32270 log`**	Denies any TCP traffic from any network from going to any network through port 32270, and logs any instance in which this statement was used
`Edge(config)#`**`access-list 152 permit ip any any`**	Allows all other traffic through
`Edge(config)#`**`interface fastethernet 0/0`**	Moves to interface configuration mode

`Edge(config-if)#ip access-group 152 in`	Takes all access list lines that are defined as being part of group 152 and applies them in an inbound manner
`Edge(config-if)#exit`	Returns to global configuration mode
`Edge(config)#interface fastethernet 0/1`	Moves to interface configuration mode
`Edge(config-if)#ip access-group 152 in`	Takes all access list lines that are defined as being part of group 152 and applies them in an inbound manner
`Edge(config-if)#exit`	Returns to global configuration mode
`Edge(config)#`	

Mitigating SubSeven

SubSeven is a backdoor Trojan horse program that targets Windows machines. When a machine is infected, the attacker can take complete control over the system and has full access as if they were a local user. Depending on the version, an attacker will try to exploit TCP ports 1243, 2773, 6711, 6712, 6713, 6776, 7000, 7215, 16959, 27374, 27573, and 54283.

Refer to Figure 5-12 for the network topology upon which the following configurations are based.

`Edge(config)#access-list 153 deny tcp any any eq 1243 log`	Denies any TCP traffic from any network from going to any network through port 1243, and logs any instance in which this statement was used
`Edge(config)#access-list 153 deny tcp any any eq 2773 log`	Denies any TCP traffic from any network from going to any network through port 2773, and logs any instance in which this statement was used

Edge(config)#**access-list 153 deny tcp any any range 6711 6713 log**	Denies any TCP traffic from any network from going to any network through ports 6711–6713, and logs any instance in which this statement was used
Edge(config)#**access-list 153 deny tcp any any eq 6776 log**	Denies any TCP traffic from any network from going to any network through port 6776, and logs any instance in which this statement was used
Edge(config)#**access-list 153 deny tcp any any eq 7000 log**	Denies any TCP traffic from any network from going to any network through port 7000, and logs any instance in which this statement was used
Edge(config)#**access-list 153 deny tcp any any eq 7215 log**	Denies any TCP traffic from any network from going to any network through port 7215, and logs any instance in which this statement was used
Edge(config)#**access-list 153 deny tcp any any eq 16959 log**	Denies any TCP traffic from any network from going to any network through port 16959, and logs any instance in which this statement was used
Edge(config)#**access-list 153 deny tcp any any eq 27374 log**	Denies any TCP traffic from any network from going to any network through port 27374, and logs any instance in which this statement was used

`Edge(config)#`**`access-list 153 deny tcp any any`** **`eq 27573 log`**	Denies any TCP traffic from any network from going to any network through port 27573, and logs any instance in which this statement was used
`Edge(config)#`**`access-list 153 deny tcp any any`** **`eq 54283 log`**	Denies any TCP traffic from any network from going to any network through port 54283, and logs any instance in which this statement was used
`Edge(config)#`**`access-list 153 permit ip any any`**	Allows all other traffic through
`Edge(config)#`**`interface fastethernet 0/0`**	Moves to interface configuration mode
`Edge(config-if)#`**`ip access-group 153 in`**	Takes all access list lines that are defined as being part of group 153 and applies them in an inbound manner
`Edge(config-if)#`**`exit`**	Returns to global configuration mode
`Edge(config)#`**`interface fastethernet 0/1`**	Moves to interface configuration mode
`Edge(config-if)#`**`ip access-group 153 in`**	Takes all access list lines that are defined as being part of group 153 and applies them in an inbound manner
`Edge(config-if)#`**`exit`**	Returns to global configuration mode
`Edge(config)#`	

Configuring an SSH Server for Secure Management and Reporting

You should use SSH instead of Telnet to manage your Cisco routers whenever possible. SSH version 1 (SSHv1) is supported in Cisco IOS Release 12.1(1)T and later, while SSH version 2 (SSHv2) is supported in Cisco IOS Release 12.3(4)T and later.

Before you can configure your routers for SSH, be sure of the following:

- Target routers are running IOS 12(1)T image or later with the IPSec feature set
- Target routers are configured for local authentication
- The AAA server is configured for username and password authentication
- Target routers all have unique hostnames
- Target routers are all using the correct domain name of your network

`Router(config)#ip domain-name yourdomain.com`	Assigns a domain name to the router
`Router(config)#crypto key generate rsa general-keys modulus 1024`	Generates an RSA key that will be used for SSH. A minimum key length of modulus 1024 is recommended.
`Router(config)#ip ssh time-out 100`	Configures the time that the router will wait for the SSH client to respond. Time is measured in seconds and can be a number from 1–120.
`Router(config)#ip ssh authentication-retries 3`	Configures the number of retires allowed. The number can range from 0–5.
`Router(config)#line vty 0 4`	Moves to line configuration mode
`Router(config-line)#no transport input telnet`	Disables Telnet on all five vty lines **NOTE:** If you are going to use SSH, be sure to disable Telnet on all router vty lines.

`Router(config-line)#transport input ssh`	Enables SSH on all five vty lines **NOTE:** Cisco routers with Cisco IOS Release 12.1(3)T and later can act as SSH clients as well as SSH servers. This means that you could initiate an SSH client-to-server session from your router to a central SSH server system.

Configuring Syslog Logging

Cisco routers are capable of logging information relating to a number of different kinds of events that occur on a router—configuration changes, ACL violations, interface status, and so on. Cisco routers can direct these log messages to several different locations: console, terminal lines, memory buffers, SNMP traps, or an external syslog server.

In order to get the most out of your router log messages, it is imperative that your routers display the correct time; using NTP will help facilitate your routers all having the correct time.

There are eight levels of severity in logging messages:

Level	Name	Definition	Example
0	emergencies	System is unusable	Cisco IOS Software could not load
1	alerts	Immediate action needed	Temperature too high
2	critical	Critical conditions	Unable to allocate memory
3	errors	Error conditions	Invalid memory size
4	warnings	Warning conditions	Crypto operation failed
5	notifications	Normal but significant conditions	Interface changed state, up or down
6	informational	Informational messages	Packet denied by ACL (default)
7	debugging	Debugging messages	Packet type invalid

Setting a level means you will get that level and everything below it. For example, level 6 means you will receive level 6 and 7 messages. Level 4 means you will get messages for levels 4–7.

`Router(config)#logging on`	Enables logging to all supported destinations
`Router(config)#logging 192.168.10.53`	Sends logging messages to a syslog server host at address 192.168.10.53
`Router(config)#logging sysadmin`	Sends logging messages to a syslog server host named sysadmin
`Router(config)#logging trap x`	Sets the syslog server logging level to value x, where x = a number between 0 and 7 or a word defining the level
`Router(config)#logging source-interface loopback 0`	Sets the source IP address of the syslog packets, regardless of the interface where the packets actually exit the router
`Router(config)#service timestamps log datetime`	Includes a timestamp in all subsequent syslog messages

Configuring an SNMP Managed Node

`Router(config)#snmp-server engineID local 1234`	Sets a string to identify the local device as 1234. If no engine ID is defined, one is generated for you.
`Router(config)#snmp-server group scottgroup v3 auth`	Defines an SNMP group named scottgroup for SNMPv3 using authentication

`Router(config)#snmp-server group hansgroup v3 auth priv`	Defines an SNMP group named hansgroup for SNMPv3 using authentication and encryption (privacy)
`Router(config)#snmp-server user Scott scottgroup v3 auth md5 scott2passwd`	Defines a user Scott belonging to the group scottgroup. Authentication uses MD5 for the password scott2passwd. No encryption parameters are set.
`Router(config)#snmp-server user Hans hansgroup v3 auth md5 hans2passwd priv des56 password2`	Defines a user Hans belonging to the group hansgroup. Authentication uses MD5 for the password hans2passwd. Encryption parameters use 56-bit DES with a password of password2.
`Router(config)#snmp-server host 172.16.31.200 inform version 3 noauth Hans`	Specifies the recipient—172.16.31.200—of an SNMP notification in the form of an inform. The SNMPv3 security level of noauth is used. The username is Hans.

Configuring NTP Clients and Servers

Use NTP to synchronize the clocks in the entire network.

`Router(config)#ntp authenticate`	Enables NTP authentication for associations with other systems
`Router(config)#ntp authentication-key 1 md5 wordpass`	Defines the authentication key as number 1, MD5 support, and a key value of wordpass **NOTE:** The key number is a number between 1–4294967295. MD5 is the only key type supported. The key value is an arbitrary value of up to eight characters.
`Router(config)#ntp trusted-key 1`	Sets the trusted key number, which must match the authentication-key number
`Router(config)#ntp server 192.168.100.15`	Configures the location of the NTP server to be found at 192.168.100.15
`Router(config)#ntp server 192.168.100.15 key 1`	Configures the location of the NTP server to be found at 192.168.100.15 and defines the authentication key as 1
`Router(config)#ntp server 192.168.100.15 key 1 prefer`	Configures the location of the NTP server to be found at 192.168.100.15 and defines the authentication key as 1 **NOTE:** The **prefer** argument states that this server is preferred over other NTP servers.

`Router(config)#interface gigabitethernet 0/0`	Moves to interface configuration mode
`Router(config-if)#ntp broadcast`	Configures this interface to send NTP broadcast packets
`Router(config-if)#ntp broadcast client`	Configures this interface to listen to NTP broadcasts
`Router(config-if)#exit`	Returns to global configuration mode
`Router(config)#access-list 1 permit host 192.168.100.15`	Creates an ACL defining a specific address of 192.168.100.15
`Router(config)#ntp access-group peer 1`	Allows time requests and NTP control queries and allows the system to synchronize itself to a system whose address passes the ACL criteria— in this case ACL 1
`Router(config)#ntp source loopback 0`	This interface is used for the source address for all packets sent to all destinations
`Router(config)#ntp peer 192.168.100.15`	Configures the router's software clock to synchronize a peer or to be synchronized by a peer at 192.168.100.15
`Router(config)#npt master 3`	Makes this system an authoritative NTP server using NTP stratum 3 **NOTE:** The stratum number is a number from 1 to 15. The default stratum is 8.

Configuration Example: NTP

Figure 5-13 shows the network topology for the configuration that follows, which shows how to configure NTP using commands covered in this chapter. Note that only the NTP commands are shown.

Figure 5-13   Network Topology for NTP Configuration Example

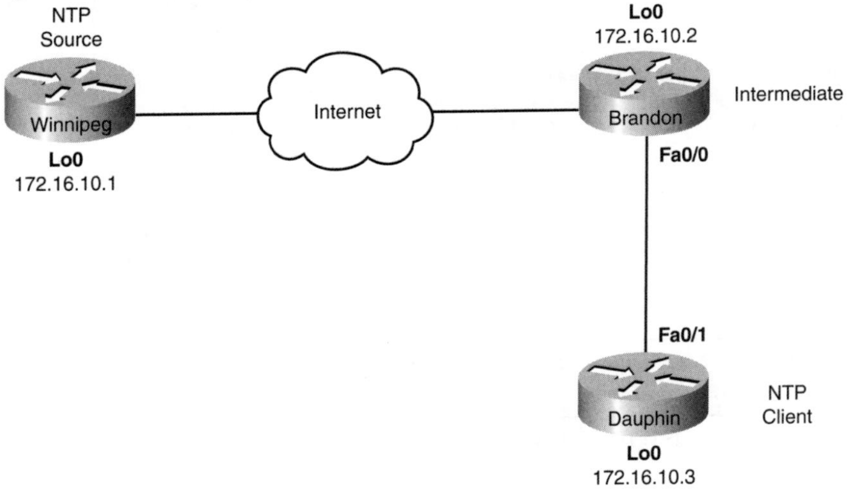

Winnipeg Router (NTP Source)

`Winnipeg(config)#ntp master 5`	Makes this system an authoritative NTP server using NTP stratum 5
`Winnipeg(config)#ntp authentication-key 1 md5 manitoba`	Creates authentication key 1 with a password of manitoba
`Winnipeg(config)#ntp peer 172.16.10.2 key 1`	Creates a peer relationship with 172.16.10.2 using authentication key 1
`Winnipeg(config)#ntp source loopback 0`	This interface is used for the source address for all packets sent to all destinations

Brandon Router (Intermediate Router)

Brandon(config)#ntp authentication-key 1 md5 manitoba	Creates authentication key 1 with a password of manitoba
Brandon(config)#ntp authentication-key 2 md5 notsask	Creates authentication key 1 with a password of notsask
Brandon(config)#ntp trusted-key 1	Defines key 1 as trusted
Brandon(config)#ntp server 172.16.10.1	Identifies the NTP server by its address of 172.16.10.1
Brandon(config)#ntp source loopback 0	This interface is used for the source address for all packets sent to all destinations
Brandon(config)#interface fastethernet 0/0	Moves to interface configuration mode
Brandon(config-if)#ntp broadcast	Configures this interface to send NTP broadcast packets

Dauphin Router (Client Router)

Dauphin(config)#ntp authentication-key 2 md5 notsask	Creates authentication key 1 with a password of notsask
Dauphin(config)#ntp trusted-key 2	Defines key 2 as trusted
Dauphin(config)#interface fastethernet 0/1	Moves to interface configuration mode
Dauphin(config-if)#ntp broadcast client	Configures this interface to listen to NTP broadcasts

Configuring AAA on Cisco Routers Using CLI

TACACS+

`Router(config)#`**`aaa new-model`**	Enables AAA with the new access control commands and thereby disables old commands
`Router(config)#`**`tacacs-server host 192.168.100.100`**	Identifies the TACACS+ server at 192.168.100.100
`Router(config)#`**`tacacs-server host 192.168.100.100 single-connection`**	Identifies the TACACS+ server at 192.168.100.100 and multiplexes all packets over a single TCP connection to the server
`Router(config)#`**`tacacs-server host 192.168.100.100 key shared1`**	Identifies the TACACS+ server at 192.168.100.100, and identifies the shared secret key of shared1
`Router(config)#`**`tacacs-server key shared1`**	Enables the shared secret encryption key shared1 between the network access server and the Cisco Secure ACS server

RADIUS

`Router(config)#aaa new-model`	Enables AAA with the new access control commands and thereby disables old commands
`Router(config)#radius-server host 192.168.100.100`	Identifies the RADIUS server at 192.168.100.100
`Router(config)#radius-server key shared1`	Enables the shared secret encryption key shared1 to be used with the RADIUS AAA server

Authentication

`Router(config)#aaa authentication login default group tacacs+ local line`	Sets the default login location as the TACACS+ server. If there is no response from the server, use the local username and password database.
`Router(config)#aaa authentication login default group radius local line`	Sets the default login location as the RADIUS server. If there is no response from the server, use the local username and password database. **NOTE:** AAA authentication can be used for general login, privileged EXEC mode access, 802.1x, EAP over UDP, PPP, and Stack Group Bidding Protocol (SGBP).

Authorization

`Router(config)#`**`aaa authorization exec default`** **`group tacacs+ local none`**	Sets that authorization will be performed by TACACS+. If no connection can be made, the local database will be used.
`Router(config)#`**`aaa authorization exec default`** **`group radius local none`**	Authorization will be performed by RADIUS. If no connection can be made, the local database will be used.
`Router(config)#`**`aaa authorization commands 15`** **`tacacs+ if-authenticated none`**	Runs authorization for all commands at privilege level 15 **NOTE:** The **aaa authorization** command can be used to authorize an EXEC shell, commands at a particular privilege level, network access (including SLIP, PPP, PPP-NCP and AppleTalk Remote Access), and reverse Telnet connections.

Accounting

`Router(config)#`**`aaa accounting exec default`** **`start-stop group tacacs+`**	Audits the EXEC process using a start-stop accounting notice with TACACS+

`Router(config)#aaa accounting network default start-stop group radius`	Audits network services using the default accounting list, using a start-stop accounting notice with RADIUS **NOTE:** The AAA accounting function can note authenticated-proxy user events, all system-level events, all network-related service requests, EXEC shell sessions, all commands at the specified privilege levels with accompanied start and stop process notices and send them to multiple AAA servers.
`Router#debug aaa authentication`	Displays information on authentication events
`Router#debug aaa authorization`	Displays information on authorization events
`Router#debug aaa accounting`	Displays information on accounting events
`Router#debug radius`	Displays information associated with RADIUS
`Router#debug tacacs`	Displays information associated with TACACS+

Configuring AAA on Cisco Routers Using SDM

From the home page of SDM, click the **Configure** button at the top of the page, and then click the **Additional Tasks** icon in the Tasks toolbar. You may need to scroll down to see the icon—it is below the NAC button. When you click the Additional Tasks icon, the window should look like the one shown in Figure 5-14.

Figure 5-14   Additional Tasks: AAA

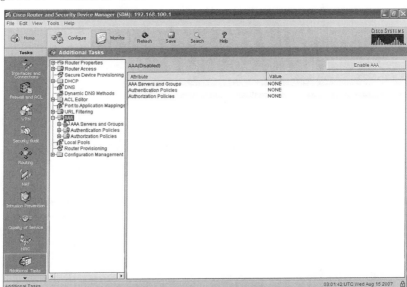

Start the AAA process by clicking the **Enable AAA** button in the upper-right part of the window. The dialog box shown in Figure 5-15 appears, telling you that SDM is going to perform some precautionary tasks before starting. Click **Yes** to continue.

Figure 5-15   Enable AAA

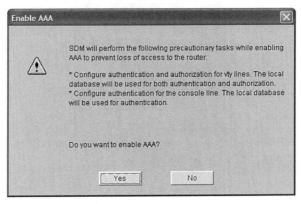

Figure 5-16 shows the Commands Delivery Status dialog box, showing that the commands needed to enable AAA have been delivered to your router.

Figure 5-16   AAA: Commands Delivery Status

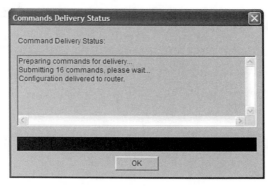

After enabling AAA on the router, you need to define an AAA server. In the Additional Tasks window (see Figure 5-14), expand **AAA** and **AAA Servers and Groups** to expose the choice of AAA Servers and AAA Groups. Click **AAA Servers** and then click the **Add** button in the upper-right corner. The Add AAA Server dialog box appears, as shown in Figure 5-17. Fill in the fields with the appropriate information and then click **OK**. Another Command Delivery Status dialog box appears. Click **OK**.

Figure 5-17   Add AAA Server

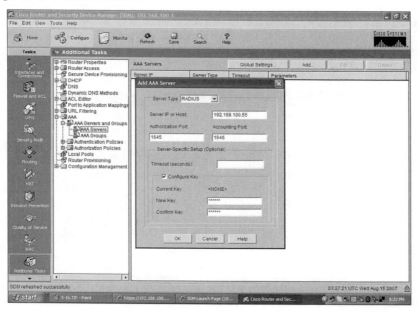

Next you have to create (or modify) an authentication policy. In the Additional Tasks window (see Figure 5-14), under AAA, expand **Authentication Policies.** You can either edit an existing policy, by highlighting it and clicking the Edit button in the upper-right corner, or create a new policy, by clicking the Add button. When AAA is enabled, a default authentication policy is created, called default, which uses local authentication to prevent session lockout. Figure 5-18 shows how to create a new policy called radius_local that will use *group radius* as the first authentication method. Note that there are several authentication methods that are available.

Figure 5-18   *Creating a Logging Authentication Policy—Group Radius*

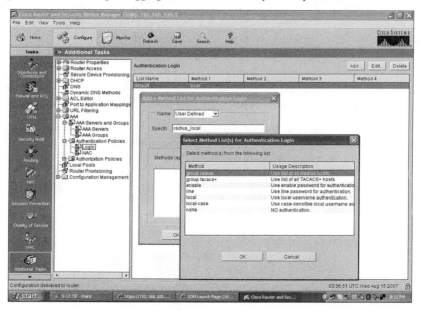

Figure 5-19 shows the addition of the *local* method as a second, backup authentication method in case RADIUS fails.

Figure 5-19   Creating a Logging Authentication Policy—Local

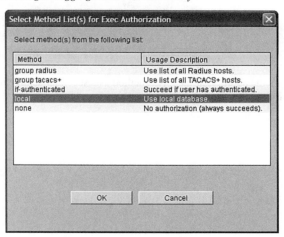

Now you need to create (or modify) an authorization policy. In the Additional Tasks window (see Figure 5-14), under AAA, expand **Authorization Policies**. You can either edit an existing policy, by highlighting it and selecting the Edit button in the upper-right corner, or create a new policy, by clicking the Add button. When AAA is enabled, a default authorization policy is created, called default. Figure 5-20 shows the creation of a new authorization policy called radius_local, which will use *group radius* as the first method for authorization, and *local* as the second, or backup method.

Figure 5-20   Creating a Logging Authorization Policy

Select Method List(s) for Exec Authorization

Select method(s) from the following list:

Method	Usage Description
group radius	Use list of all Radius hosts.
group tacacs+	Use list of all TACACS+ hosts.
if-authenticated	Succeed if user has authenticated.
local	Use local database.
none	No authorization (always succeeds).

OK   Cancel

After creating local authentication in the AAA configuration on the router, you need to add user accounts to the local database. In the Additional Tasks window, expand **Router Access** and select **User Accounts/View**. Click **Add**, and you see the Add an Account dialog box, shown in Figure 5-21. Enter in all appropriate information such as username, password, password encryption if required, and associated privilege level, if required. Click the OK button when finished. If you want to add another user account, click **ADD** again and repeat the process.

Figure 5-21   Adding an Account

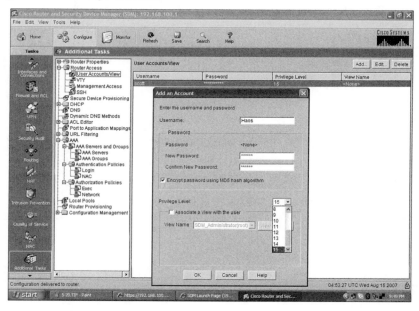

CHAPTER 6

Cisco IOS Threat Defense Features

This chapter provides information and commands concerning the following topics:

- Configuring an IOS Firewall from the command-line interface (CLI)
- Configuring a Basic Firewall using Secure Device Manager (SDM)
- Configuring an Advanced Firewall using SDM
- Verifying firewall activity using the CLI
- Verifying firewall activity using SDM
- Configuring a Cisco IOS Intrusion Prevention System (IPS) from the CLI
- Configuring a Cisco IOS IPS from the SDM
- Viewing Security Device Event Exchange (SDEE) messages through SDM
- Tuning signatures through SDM

Configuring an IOS Firewall from the CLI

Figure 6-1 shows the network topology for the configuration that follows, which shows how to configure a Cisco IOS Firewall from the command-line interface (CLI).

Figure 6-1 Network Topology for IOS Firewall CLI Configuration

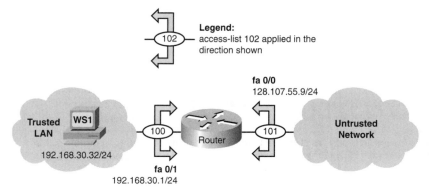

The six steps to implementing a Cisco IOS Firewall from the CLI follow:

Step 1.   Choose the interface and packet direction to inspect.

Step 2.   Configure an IP ACL for the interface.

Step 3.   Set audit trails and alerts.

Step 4.   Define the inspection rules.

Step 5.   Apply the inspection rules and the ACL to the outside interface.

Step 6.   Verify the configuration.

Following the presentation of these steps, this section lists and describes commands for troubleshooting the configuration.

Step 1: Choose the Interface and Packet Direction to Inspect

Choose inbound LAN traffic at FastEthernet 0/1 to the untrusted network for ACL 100. The direction of traffic is relative to the router. Choose inbound WAN traffic at FastEthernet 0/1 for ACL 101. ACL 101 permits traffic from the untrusted network that is not specifically handled by the stateful inspection outbound at FastEthernet 0/1.

Step 2: Configure an IP ACL for the Interface

Router(config)# **accesslist 100 permit tcp 192.168.30.0 0.0.0.255 any**	Allows inside legitimate traffic and prevents spoofing
Router(config)# **accesslist 100 permit udp 192.168.30.0 0.0.0.255 any**	Allows inside legitimate traffic and prevents spoofing
Router(config)# **accesslist 100 permit icmp 192.168.30.0 0.0.0.255 any**	Allows inside legitimate traffic and prevents spoofing
Router(config)# **accesslist 100 deny ip any any**	Allows inside legitimate traffic and prevents spoofing
Router(config)#**access-list 101 deny ip 192.168.30.0 0.0.0.255 any**	Denies a spoofed address (192.168.30.x/24)
Router(config)#**access-list 101 permit icmp any host 128.107.55.9 echo-reply**	Permits returning ICMP echo reply
Router(config)#**access-list 101 permit icmp any host 128.107.55.9 time-exceeded**	Permits returning ICMP time-exceeded message
Router(config)#**access-list 101 permit icmp any host 128.107.55.9 unreachable**	Permits returning ICMP host unreachable message
Router(config)#**access-list 101 deny ip 10.0.0.0 0.255.255.255 any**	Denies public IP 10.0.0.0/8

Router(config)#**access-list 101 deny ip 172.16.0.0 0.15.255.255 any**	Denies public IP 172.16.0.0/12
Router(config)#**access-list 101 deny ip 192.168.0.0 0.0.255.255 any**	Denies public IP 192.168.0.0/16
Router(config)#**access-list 101 deny ip 127.0.0.0 0.255.255.255 any**	Denies traffic from the loopback address
Router(config)#**access-list 101 deny ip host 255.255.255.255 any**	Denies any broadcast
Router(config)#**access-list 101 deny ip 0.0.0.0 0.255.255.255 any**	Denies traffic from any device with a source address of 0.x.x.x
Router(config)#**access-list 101 deny ip any any log**	Denies all other traffic and logs the results **NOTE:** Context-Based Access Control (CBAC) setup is provided in the following steps.

Step 3: Set Audit Trails and Alerts

Router(config)#**logging on**	Enables the logging service
Router(config)#**logging host 192.168.30.33**	Sets the syslog server IP address
Router(config)#**ip inspect audit-trail**	Turns on CBAC audit trail messages, which are displayed on the console
Router(config)#**ip inspect dns-timeout 7**	Specifies the DNS idle timeout (default is 5 seconds)
Router(config)#**ip inspect tcp idle-time 14400**	Specifies the TCP idle timeout (default is 3600 seconds)

| Router(config)#**ip inspect udp idle-time 1800** | Specifies the UDP idle timeout (default is 30 seconds) |
| Router(config)#**no ip inspect alert-off** | Enables real-time alerts

NOTE: Cisco IOS Firewall real-time alerts are off by default (the command **ip inspect alert-off** is active by default). To enable real-time alerts, the **no** version of the command is needed; use the **no ip inspect alert-off** command in global configuration mode. |

Step 4: Define the Inspection Rules

NOTE: To override the global TCP, UDP, or Internet Control Message Protocol (ICMP) idle timeouts for the specified protocol, specify the number of seconds for a different idle timeout in the **ip inspect name** command.

Router(config)#**ip inspect name INSPECTION-RULE tftp timeout 20**	Instructs the router to inspect protocol TFTP with 20-second idle timeout
Router(config)#**ip inspect name INSPECTION-RULE udp timeout 15**	Instructs the router to inspect protocol UDP with 15-second idle timeout
Router(config)#**ip inspect name INSPECTION-RULE tcp timeout 600**	Instructs the router to inspect protocol TCP with 600-second idle timeout
Router(config)#**ip inspect name INSPECTION-RULE ftp timeout 600**	Instructs the router to inspect protocol FTP with 600-second idle timeout

`Router(config)#ip inspect name INSPECTION-RULE http timeout 600`	Instructs the router to inspect protocol HTTP with 600-second idle timeout
`Router(config)#ip inspect name INSPECTION-RULE smtp alert on audit-trail on timeout 300`	Instructs the router to inspect protocol SMTP, turns on alert messages, turns on the audit trail, and sets the timeout to 300 seconds **NOTE:** For both the **alert** and **audit-trail** arguments, if there is no option selected, alerts or messages will be generated based on the setting of the **ip inspect alert-off** command or the **ip inspect audit-trail** command.

Step 5: Apply the Inspection Rules and the ACL to the Outside Interface

`Router(config)#interface fastethernet 0/1`	Moves to interface configuration mode
`Router(config-if)#ip access-group 100 in`	Applies ACL 100 to this interface, which permits the specified traffic through the router to the untrusted network
`Router(config)#interface fastethernet 0/0`	Moves to interface configuration mode
`Router(config-if)#ip inspect INSPECTION-RULE out`	Instructs the router to maintain stateful session information for protocols named in INSPECTION-RULE for outbound traffic

`Router(config-if)#ip access-group 101 in`	Permits inbound traffic not specifically handled by the CBAC **NOTE:** Inbound traffic not handled by the CBAC must be specifically permitted inbound at the outside WAN interface (ACL 101). All other protocols specified in the CBAC inspection rule will be "pinholed" through the firewall when there is a session match to the outbound requesting traffic (stateful inspection).

Step 6: Verify the Configuration

`Router#show ip inspect name INSPECTION-RULE`	Displays information about the inspection rule named INSPECTION-RULE
`Router#show ip inspect config`	Displays information about inspection configuration
`Router#show ip inspect interfaces`	Displays information about inspection interfaces
`Router#show ip inspect session`	Displays information about inspection sessions (use the **detail** argument for added information)
`Router#show ip inspect statistics`	Displays information about inspection statistics
`Router#show ip inspect all`	Displays all available inspection information

Troubleshooting the Configuration

Router#**debug ip inspect function-trace**	Displays messages about software functions that the firewall calls
Router#**debug ip inspect object-creation**	Displays messages about created software objects
Router#**debug ip inspect object-deletion**	Displays messages about deleted software objects
Router#**debug ip inspect events**	Displays messages about software events and packet processing
Router#**debug ip inspect timers**	Displays messages about timer events
Router#**debug ip inspect detailed**	Displays detailed information for all other enabled debugging
Router#**debug ip inspect** *protocol*	Displays messages about the specific protocol defined in the command

Configuring a Basic Firewall Using SDM

As shown in Figure 6-2, from the home page of Cisco Router and Security Device Manager (SDM), click the **Configure** button at the top of the page, and then click the **Firewall and ACL** icon in the Tasks toolbar on the left. You have two choices: Basic Firewall and Advanced Firewall. Click the **Basic Firewall** radio button and then click the **Launch the Selected Task** button to proceed to the Basic Firewall Configuration Wizard.

Figure 6-2   *Launching the Basic Firewall Configuration Wizard*

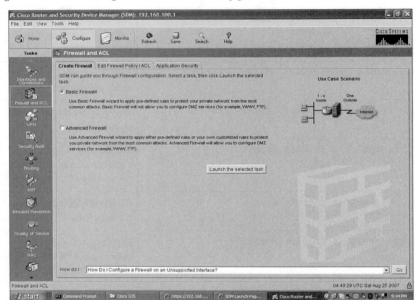

Note that you must have two interfaces configured with IP addresses in order to run this wizard. If you do not, you will be given an Information dialog box like the one shown in Figure 6-3. If this happens, you must go back and configure two interfaces before continuing.

Figure 6-3   *Two Interfaces Configured with IP Required*

Figure 6-4 shows the start of the Basic Firewall Configuration Wizard. Click **Next** to continue.

Figure 6-4   *Basic Firewall Configuration Wizard*

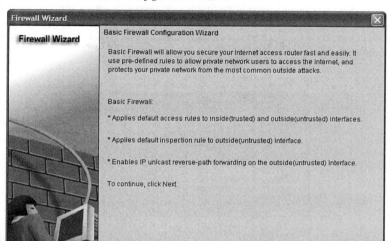

On the next page of the wizard, shown in Figure 6-5, identify your inside and outside interfaces. You can have more than one inside (trusted) interface, and you have the choice of allowing secure SDM access from your outside interfaces.

Figure 6-5   *Specifying Outside and Inside Interfaces*

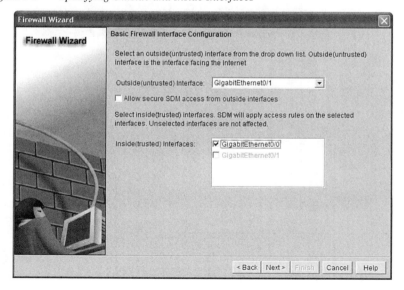

After you click **Next** to proceed to the next window, you receive a warning, shown in Figure 6-6, that you cannot launch SDM through the outside interface after the wizard completes. In this example, GigabitEthernet 0/1 is the outside interface. Ensure that you are not using your outside interface to access SDM and then click **OK** to continue to the next step of the wizard.

Figure 6-6   Configuration Warning

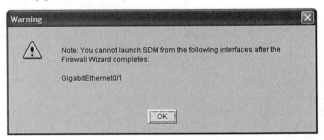

Figure 6-7 shows the final page of the wizard, the Internet Firewall Configuration Summary. Note that the wizard has created access rules to both the inside and outside interfaces to set up the firewall. Click **Finish** to complete the wizard, or click **Back** to return to the wizard to make any configuration changes.

Figure 6-7   Internet Firewall Configuration Summary—Basic Firewall

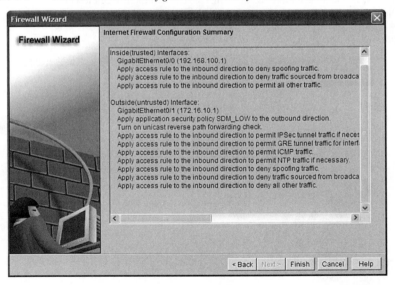

Figure 6-8 shows the Edit Firewall Policy/ACL tab, where you can verify and customize your firewall settings, such as adding, editing, or deleting applications or adding, editing, or deleting services.

Figure 6-8   Edit Firewall Policy/ACL Tab

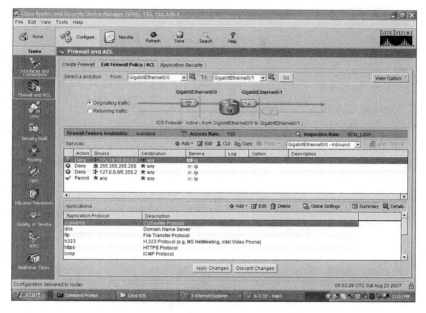

Configuring an Advanced Firewall Using SDM

As shown in Figure 6-9, from the home page of SDM, click the **Configure** button at the top of the page, and then click the **Firewall and ACL** icon in the Tasks toolbar. You have two choices: Basic Firewall and Advanced Firewall. Click the **Advanced Firewall** radio button and then click the **Launch the Selected Task** button to proceed to the next window, shown in Figure 6-10.

Figure 6-9   Launching the Advanced Firewall Configuration Wizard

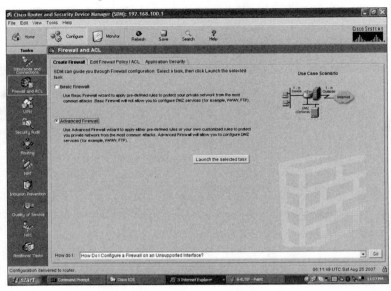

Figure 6-10   Advanced Firewall Configuration Wizard

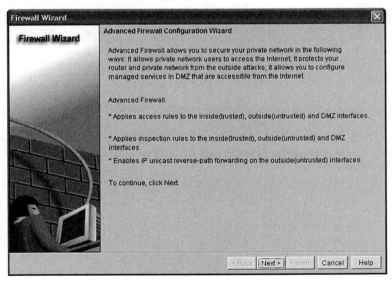

Like the Basic Firewall Configuration Wizard, the Advanced Firewall Configuration Wizard also prompts you to choose your inside and outside interfaces, along with SDM access from your outside interfaces. If required, you can also define an interface for your DMZ, as demonstrated in Figure 6-11. Click **Next**, and a warning about launching SDM from an outside interface appears, similar to the one shown in the Basic Firewall Configuration Wizard (refer to Figure 6-6). Click **OK** to continue.

Figure 6-11   Advanced Firewall Interface Configuration

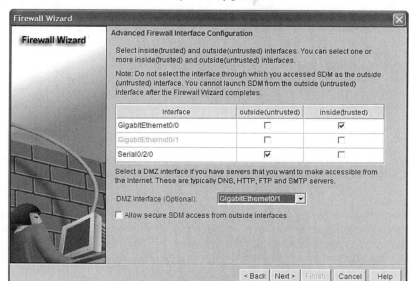

If you have selected an interface as a DMZ interface, you are shown the Advanced Firewall DMZ Service Configuration window, as shown in Figure 6-12. In this window, you can define DMZ services that are accessible from the outside network, such as mail, FTP, and VPN. Click **Add** to define a DMZ service.

Figure 6-12   Advanced Firewall DMZ Service Configuration

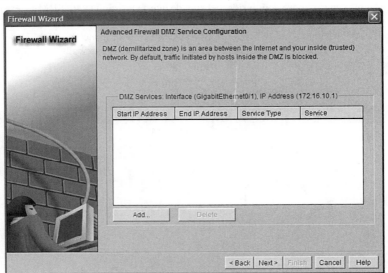

Figure 6-13 shows the DMZ Service Configuration dialog box. Enter the IP address of the server, followed by the service port number or well-known name. Clicking the ellipsis button opens the Service Menu where you can select the service from a list of well-known services. If you open this menu, click **OK** to return to the DMZ Service Configuration dialog box. After you have entered in all of the DMZ services required, click **Next** to continue.

Figure 6-13   DMZ Service Configuration and Service Dialog Boxes

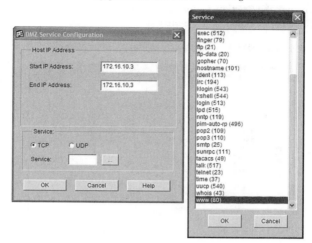

The next item to configure is the inspection granularity for services that are running in the DMZ. Figure 6-14 shows that you have the option of choosing a default SDM Application Security Policy or choosing a custom Application Security Policy.

Figure 6-14   Advanced Firewall Security Configuration—Using a Default Policy

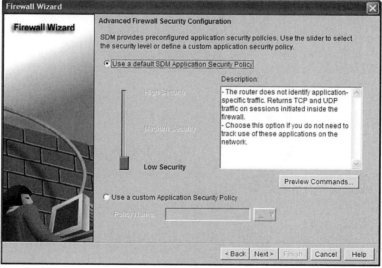

If you use a default policy, click the **Use a Default SDM Application Security Policy** radio button and then click the **Preview Commands** button to see which specific configuration commands will be applied (shown in Figure 6-15).

Figure 6-15   Preview SDM Application Security Policy

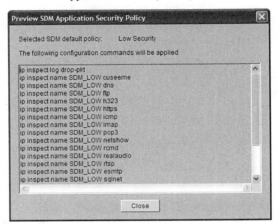

If you choose to use a custom policy, you can either create a new policy or select an existing policy, as shown in Figure 6-16. Click **Create a New Policy** to open the Application Security window, shown in Figure 6-17, where you can choose the applications that should be inspected by the firewall.

Figure 6-16   Creating a New Custom Application Security Policy

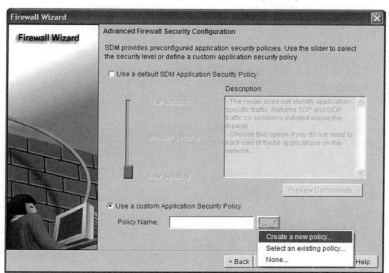

Figure 6-17   Application Security Inspection

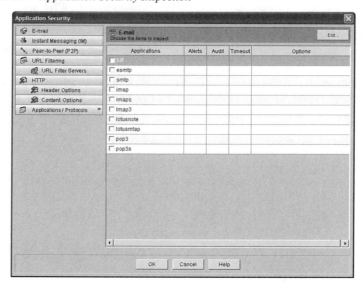

The parameters of each protocol can be modified by checking the box next to the protocol and clicking the Edit button in the upper-right corner of the window. As shown in Figure 6-18, you can modify alerts, audits, and timeouts. Depending on the protocol, you might be able to choose whether local router traffic should also be inspected by checking the Router Traffic check box.

Figure 6-18   Edit Inspection Rule Dialog Box

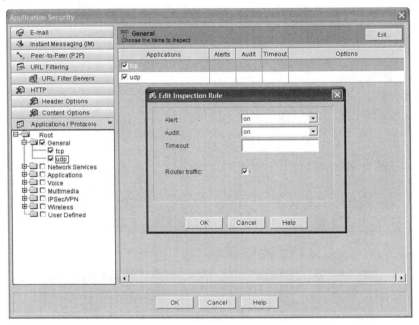

When you finish choosing protocols and modifying the parameters, click **OK** to continue. You are returned to the Advanced Firewall Security Configuration Wizard page, where you can select which security policy you want to use on this router, as shown in Figure 6-19. The router produced a default name for the custom policy that you just created. Click **Next** to use this policy and proceed to the next wizard page.

Figure 6-19   Advanced Firewall Security Configuration—Using a Custom Policy

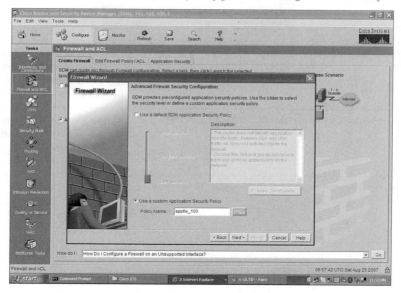

Figure 6-20 shows the last page of the wizard, the Internet Firewall Configuration Summary. This window lists all firewall rules that will be applied to this router. Click **Finish** to apply the configuration to the router.

Figure 6-20   Internet Firewall Configuration Summary—Advanced Firewall

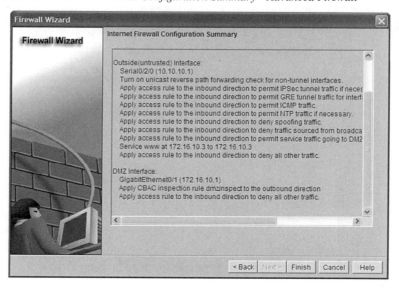

Verifying Firewall Activity Using CLI

To verify the router configuration using the CLI, use the following commands.

Router#**show running-config** | **include ip inspect** *name*	Displays only the lines in the running configuration that contain the string **ip inspect** *name*
Router#**show running-config** | **include access-list**	Displays only the lines in the running configuration that contain the string **access-list**
Router#**show running-config** | **begin interface**	Displays the running configuration beginning at the first instance of the word interface

Verifying Firewall Activity Using SDM

To activate logging using SDM, click the **Configure** button at the top of the SDM home page, and then click the **Additional Tasks** icon in the Tasks toolbar. In the Additional Tasks window, expand **Router Properties** and click **Logging**. The Logging window appears, as shown in Figure 6-21.

Figure 6-21   Logging

To modify your logging settings, click the **Edit** button in the upper-right corner of the window. Choose the Logging Level you want, as shown in Figure 6-22, and click **OK**.

Figure 6-22   Logging Level

After firewall logging has been activated, you can view the firewall log by clicking the **Monitor** icon in the top navigation bar, clicking the **Logging** icon in the Tasks toolbar on the left, and clicking the **Firewall Log** tab, as shown in Figure 6-23.

Figure 6-23   Firewall Log

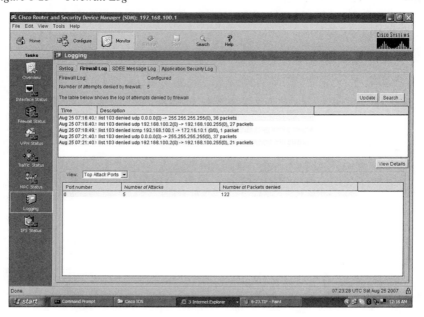

Configuring Cisco IOS Intrusion Prevention System from the CLI

Cisco IOS can act as an inline intrusion detection sensor, watching packets as they flow through the router and scanning them to match anything from a Cisco IOS Intrusion Prevention System (IPS) signature. If the IPS detects suspicious activity, it can respond before the network can be compromised. A log of the event is then recorded through either syslog or the Security Device Event Exchange (SDEE) protocol.

Starting with Cisco IOS Release 12.4(11)T, Cisco IOS IPS introduces support for the Cisco IPS Software Version 5.x signature format, which is also used by other Cisco appliance-based IPS products. The Cisco IPS version 5.x signature format is improved to support encrypted signature parameters and other features such as signature Risk Rating.

Cisco Signature Definition Files (SDF) are updated and posted on Cisco.com. Default SDF files are shipped with routers, and larger ones that contain more signatures can be downloaded. Select the appropriate SDF file based on the amount of RAM in the router.

There are five steps to configure and verify a basic Cisco IOS IPS:

Step 1.   Specify the location of the SDF.

Step 2.   Configure the failure parameter.

Step 3.   Create an IPS rule and optionally apply an ACL.

Step 4.   Apply the IPS rule to an interface.

Step 5.   Verify the IPS configuration.

Step 1: Specify the Location of the SDF

`Router(config)#ip ips sdf builtin`	Specifies to use the built-in SDF **NOTE:** The **ip ids sdf builtin** command does not appear in the configuration file because it is the default command. This command appears in the file only if a nondefault SDF is used.
`Router(config)#ip ips sdf location flash:/ips5`	Specifies to use the SDF located in the folder named ips5 located in flash **NOTE:** To create the directory for the location of the nondefault SDF, use the **mkdir** command from privileged mode: `Router#mkdir flash:/ ips` The SDF file can be located on the root of flash (flash:) if so desired.

Step 2: Configure the Failure Parameter

`Router(config)#ip ips fail closed`	Specifies to not forward traffic if a System Microengine (SME) fails **NOTE:** If the SME fails, and you still want to forward packets without scanning, remove this command with the **no ip ips fail closed** command.

Step 3: Create an IPS Rule, and Optionally Apply an ACL

`Router(config)#`**`ip ips name ROUTER-IPS`**	Creates an IPS rule named ROUTER-IPS
`Router(config)#`**`ip ips name TEST-IPS list 123`**	Creates an IPS rule named TEST-IPS and applies ACL 123 for further scrutiny of scanned packets

Step 4: Apply the IPS Rule to an Interface

`Router(config)#`**`interface fastethernet 0/0`**	Moves to interface configuration mode
`Router(config)#`**`ip virtual-reassembly`**	Virtually reassembles fragments so packets can be scanned by the IPS **NOTE:** Cisco suggests that the **ip virtual-reassembly** command be applied to all interfaces where traffic comes into the router, to facilitate the IPS engines.
`Router(config-if)#`**`ip ips ROUTER-IPS in`**	Applies the IPS rule at the interface, loads the signatures, and builds the signature engines **NOTE:** This process can take up to 10 minutes depending on the router platform. It is recommended that you enable logging messages to monitor the engine building status.

NOTE: Enable logging with the following commands.

`Router(config)#logging on`	Enables logging to all supported destinations
`Router(config)#logging 192.168.10.53`	Sends logging messages to a syslog server host at address 192.168.10.53
`Router(config)#logging sysadmin`	Sends logging messages to a syslog server host named *sysadmin*

Step 5: Verify the IPS Configuration

`Router(config)#exit`	Returns to global configuration mode
`Router#show ip ips configuration`	Verifies that the IOS IPS is properly configured
`Router#show ip ips signature`	Verifies the number of signatures that are loaded into each SME

IPS Enhancements

Several enhancements that are possible with an IPS configuration follow:

- Merge SDFs
- Disable, delete, and filter selected signatures within an SDF
- Change the location of the SDF

Merge SDFs

`Router#copy flash:attack-drop.sdf ips.sdf`	Merges the attack-drop.sdf file with the default SDF stored in memory
`Router#copy ips.sdf flash:newsignatures.sdf`	Creates a new SDF in flash that can now be used when the router boots

`Router#configure terminal`	Moves to global configuration mode
`Router(config)#ip ips sdf location flash:newsignatures.sdf`	Modifies the location of the SDF **NOTE:** This location must be changed before any modifications to the SDF can be performed.

Disable, Delete, and Filter Selected Signatures Within an SDF

`Router(config)#ip ips signature 1107 0 disable`	Deactivates the signature with ID 1107 and subsignature 0. The signature remains in the SDF; it is just deactivated.
`Router(config)#ip ips signature 5037 0 delete`	Deletes the signature with ID 5037 and subsignature 0. The signature is removed from the SDF the next time the signatures are reloaded or saved.
`Router(config)#ip ips signature 6190 0 list 145`	Applies ACL 145 to signature 6190, subsignature 0 for specific packet scanning

Change the Location of the SDF

`Router(config)#ip ips name NEW-IPS list 123`	Creates an IPS rule named NEW-IPS and applies ACL 123 for further scrutiny of scanned packets
`Router(config)#interface fastethernet 0/0`	Moves to interface configuration mode

`Router(config-if)#ip ips NEW-IPS in`	Applies the IPS rule at the interface, loads the signatures, and builds the signature engines **NOTE:** The original IPS name ROUTER-IPS could be used, but the `ip ips name` command must be executed again to map the new SDF into the IPS. If the original IPS name is remapped, it does not need to be reapplied to the interface.

Configuring Cisco IOS IPS from the SDM

SDM provides a useful set of wizards to configure IPS. To access these wizards, click the **Configure** button on the top of the SDM home page, and then click the **Intrusion Prevention** icon in the Tasks toolbar to display the window shown in Figure 6-24.

Figure 6-24   Intrusion Prevention System Home Page

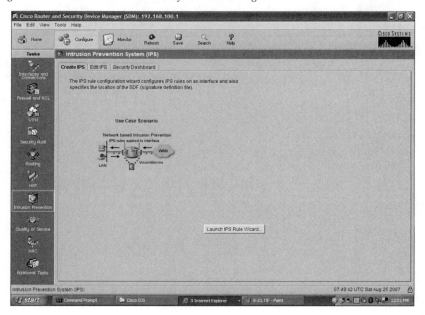

Ensure that the Create IPS tab is shown. To activate IPS with the default signature parameters, click the **Launch IPS Rule Wizard** button to display the window in Figure 6-25. Click **Next** to proceed to the Select Interfaces page, shown in Figure 6-26, which allows you to choose the interfaces as well as the direction in which IPS rules will be applied.

Figure 6-25   IPS Policies Wizard

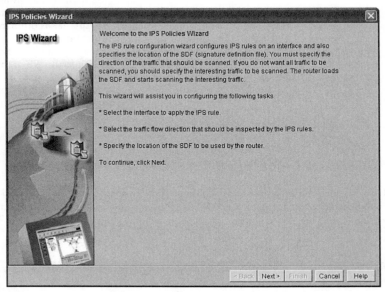

Figure 6-26   Select Interfaces—No Interfaces or Directions Chosen

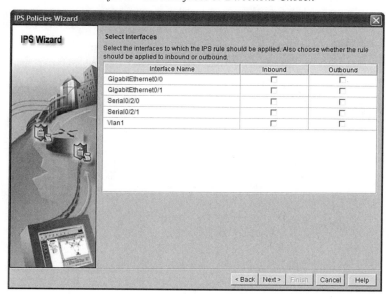

After you have chosen your interfaces and the appropriate direction (inbound or outbound), as shown in Figure 6-27, the IPS should be applied. Click **Next** to advance to the SDF Locations page, shown in Figure 6-28.

Figure 6-27   Select Interfaces—Interface and Direction Chosen

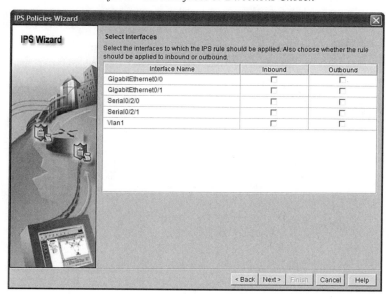

Figure 6-28   SDF Locations

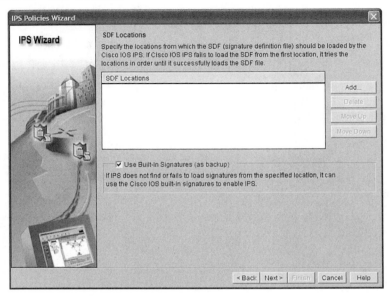

From the SDF Locations page, you can click the Add button to add a signature location. You can also use a built-in signature as a backup. The built-in signature is enabled by default; uncheck the check box if you do not wish to do this. Figure 6-29 shows the dialog box that appears for you to add a signature location. After you specify the SDF location, click **OK** to be returned to the SDF Location page, and then click **Next** to continue. A summary page will appear. Click **Finish** to apply the rule to the router, as shown in Figure 6-30.

Figure 6-29   Add a Signature Location

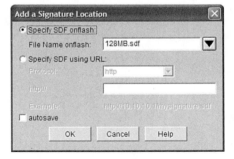